Guidelines on Fundamentalism and Theological Education

Guidelines on Fundamentalism and Theological Education

H. G. Mithra
Israel Selvanayagam

The Association of Theological Teachers in India
(ATTI)
&
Christian World Imprints™

First Published in 2017 by

Association of Theological Teachers in India (ATTI)
thru **Rev. Dr. H. G. Mithra, Secretary, ATTI**
Union Biblical Seminary
PUNE 411037 / MAHARASHTRA
hid3_mithra@rediffmail.com
Phone: 09421200718

&

Christian World Imprints™
Christian Publishing & Books from India
H-12 Bali Nagar, New Delhi-110015
info@christianworldimprints.com
www.ChristianWorldImprints.com
Phone: +91 11 25465925

ISBN: 978-93-5148-242-0 (HB) ISBN: 978-93-5148-243-7 (PB)

Cataloging in Publication Data--DK
Courtesy: D.K. Agencies (P) Ltd. <docinfo@dkagencies.com>

Mithra, H. G., author.
Guidelines on fundamentalism and theological education / H.G. Mithra, Israel Selvanayagam.
pages cm
ISBN 9789351482420 (HB)
ISBN 9789351482437 (PB)

1. Fundamentalism--India. 2. Theology--Study and teaching--India. I. Celvanāyakam, Israyēl, author. II. Association of Theological Teachers in India, publisher. III. Title.

LCC BT82.2.M58 2017 | DDC 270.82 23

Printed in India

Contents

Preface

Fundamentalism is a growing threat for the truly religious and those committed to maintain and enhance human welfare and development. Therefore, it is important to understand its dynamics and effects internationally, nationally, regionally and locally. Theological education helps those who are open to learn and change from any form of fundamentalism to the true fundamentals of their faith. Despite some overlap, each religious tradition has its own fundamentalism. The minority Christian fundamentalism in India is seen to have triggered greater and dangerous manifestations of other major religions in the multifaith India. It is hard to deny that the fundamentalist Christians in India have been influenced by the fundamentalist movement of the West, particularly the United States of America. There is hardly any awareness of the resources and challenges of the multi-religious and multi-cultural India. Theological education is supposed to equip people and ministers in the fundamentals of the Christian faith (e.g. love, justice, peace and the power of powerlessness). But there is no guarantee that the popular and formal form of theological education can make an adequate response to fundamentalism. In fact, an empirical study might suggest that some theological institutions and their staff are fundamentalist in their outlook due to various compulsions though they appear to be academic.

The Association of Theological Teachers in India (ATTI) which started in late 1970s has been providing opportunities for theological teachers, based in about sixty theological institutions affiliated to the Senate of Serampore College (University) all over India for forming fraternity and sharing concerns. From time to time it has organized conferences for discussing themes that are relevant to the Indian situation. For example,papers presented in a national consultation of the ATTI in 1981 was published: Gnana Robinson, Henry Wilson and Christopher Duraisingh (eds.), *Theological Education and Development: Papers Presented at the National Theological Teachers Conference April,1981* (Bangalore: The Association of Theological Teachers in India, 1984). When the ATTI was revived during 2013-2016, the members of the Executive Committee proposed to organize conferences and consultations. One of us (IS) was authorized to explore possibilities of resources for holding a conference on 'Religion and Secularity in India' for theological teachers in general, and a consultation on 'The challenges of fundamentalism and implications for theological education in India' for Principals of the colleges/ seminaries in particular. Both were held one after another during 4-8 August 2015 at the Henry Martyn Institute, Hyderabad. The HMI, which has the track record of moving from direct evangelism among Muslims, to study of Islam in an objective manner and of late to focusing on peace and reconciliation, came forward to offer collaboration for running both the events.

Let us concentrate here on the consultation on fundamentalism for the Principals. Apart from HMI's collaboration, the Board for Theological Education of the Senate of Serampore College (BTESSC), impressed by the proposal, granted a bursary from its 'Solidarity Fund.' Still we needed an additional bursary which specifically was for the publication of the 'Guidelines.' The Trustees of the Teape Foundation at Cambridge came forward to support with a bursary. Thus, it has been a collaborative effort involving many. We want to place on record our appreciation and gratitude for all our colleagues and friends for their generous contributions. They include the Director (Dt. Packiam Samuel) and staff members of the HMI.

Due to some uncertainties and other reasons many of the Principals were not able to come. But those ten who came along, with the organisers and some guests, discussed intensively the nature and manifestations of fundamentalism in the Indian Church. The discussions were guided by a major presentation of one of us (IS) and five more short presentations by the participants. An outline for the 'Guidelines' was agreed. We then shared our responsibility of drafting them – one (IS) doing the initial drafting and the other (GHM) checking, commenting and agreeing. We sent the draft to all the participants. The comments and corrections were incorporated. We have deliberately avoided bringing in the scientific criticisms of the Bible. We believe that there are more than sufficient reasons to point out in the Bible itself for a careful and fruitful reading, which will be corrective of popular misunderstanding. It is our hope and prayer that these guidelines will be read and discussed in churches and theological institutions. We encourage translation of it in different vernaculars.

We place on record with immense gratitude to William Allberry, a visiting teacher of English at Tamilnadu Theological Seminary, Madurai, for correcting and polishing the language and making most valuable comments.

The publisher (Christian World Imprints) deserves our thankful appreciation for kind dealing and likeable presentation.

Israel Selvanayagam
Evesham, UK

H. G. Mithra
Pune, India

Introduction

George Ninan (1934-2015) a former bishop in the Church of North India, who promoted social engagement of addressing urban issues, once observed that more than 90% of Indian Christians are fundamentalists. Literal or twisted interpretation of one's or a group's favourite biblical verses is basic to scriptural fundamentalism. Where there is a lack of balance and integration it leads to fundamentalism. For example, one may construct the Christian story without any regard for the root story of liberation of the Hebrew slaves in Egypt and continued liberation with the contributions of prophets. Jesus could be detached from the Hebrew line of liberation and prophecy because of his missionary alignment to the Greek and Roman traditions. Without approaching the mystical and mysterious union of the triune Godhead Christians may drift to a Jesus cult or Spirit experience. Instead of seeking union for the sake of effective witness, there may be denominational rigidity and sectarian proliferation. Although the Bible presents a profound vision of integrated personality and holistic salvation, churches and charismatic/sectarian groups in India are pre-occupied with a soul winning activity with the centrality of 'cleansing by the blood of Jesus' and promise of a glorious after life. These and other factors have been pointed out by those who have sacrificed their life for realizing a holistic view of life and mission, like bishop George Ninian.

The word 'fundamentalism' originated in the USA in the 1920s and it has a particular background. In 1909, two wealthy Christian business brothers 'set aside a large sum of money for issuing twelve volumes that would set forth the fundamentals of the Christian faith. These were to be sent free to ministers of the gospel, missionaries, Sunday School superintendents, and others engaged in aggressive Christian work throughout the English- speaking world. A committee of men of sound faith was set up to have oversight of the publication of these volumes. As planned, twelve volumes were brought out between 1910 and 1915. They were sent to about 300,000 of the above mentioned in different parts of the world.' The common title of these booklets was *The Fundamentals: A Testimony to the Truth.* Later editions have been produced in different combinations.

The above plan was in response to the challenge of the sweeping influence of modern higher criticism of the Bible and new scientific theories such as evolution that appeared to shatter the age long certainties of Christian believers. But they were not of the fundamentalists of later types associated with terrorism, militancy and bigotry. Nor were they sectarians of an exotic type and even today those who subscribe to the views of the above booklets cannot accept other groups with similar commitment and concerns. While all of them were enthusiastic to commend the Christian message to all people they hardly had the sensitivity about minority Christians living in multi-faith and multi-cultural contexts such as India.

The fundamentalist influence was widespread and varied in the USA. However, there have been extreme movements with cult leaders. Most notable is Jim Jones, the cult leader of 'Peoples Temple', who led more than nine hundred followers in a mass suicide on 18 November 1978. As he was typical of some cult or charismatic leaders we give a summary of the background and painful episode. After a period of struggle in his life Jones claimed to have found the way and joined as a student pastor at a Methodist church in Indianapolis in 1952. In the following year, he made a reputation as a healer and evangelist. In 1955 he branched out on his own forming 'Wing of Deliverance Church' which soon came to be known as the 'Peoples Temple.' He started publishing newsletters and magazines and bought time on a local radio station to air his sermons and healing powers. As self-proclaimed Messiah, he promised utopia for his followers. He moved to California with about a hundred of his male followers. With dark glasses, suits, lock hair and particular style of holding the Bible he appeared impressive at pulpits. Soon he turned to be paranoid and contradictory. For example, he discouraged sex and romantic relationship, but he had several adulterous relationships that resulted in the birth of some children. In 1974 he bought a land in Gayana and when life became unpleasant he moved to Peoples Temple compound with about a thousand followers and named it Jonestown. He forced an austere life that created ill feelings. Fearing a plot against his life, he conducted suicide drills and threatened the government and critics with mass suicide. Investigators were sent and they were attacked and killed by his men, and some defectors also fell victims. Finally, he called for his 'revolutionary suicide' campaign (probably asserting the end of times). Cyanide and Valium were mixed to make a toxic punch and served almost as a sacramental wine and forced on those who refused. Of the nine hundred dead two hundred and seventy- six were children. Jim Jones was later found dead with a gun shot in his head.

The alarming and shocking episode of Jim Jones helped the critics to reinforce the idea that religion is 'a poisoned chalice.' Excluding the mass murder, the other aspects of Jim Jones' approach are evident in the 'evangelical ministry' of sectarian movements and independent preachers around the world. In India, fundamentalist movements and preachers are very successful in terms of attracting people by the strategic use of mass media and agents and amassing wealth. Running magazines, buying radio and TV times, and giving flashing publicity, they propagate their labels and special thrusts. The typical captions for their healing campaigns are 'the blind see, lame walk, deaf hear and blessings rain.' It often works in hierarchical forms. For instance, at the time of tragic or premature death the spouse or the family take up the ministry even though they lack the charisma of the founder. Few manage to establish institutions which become commercial and only an empirical research will reveal if the route has been clean or involving usual corrupt means, particularly with the authorities.

Individual salvation by dipping in the blood of Jesus is the central message of the fundamentalist groups. Then comes the experience of being filled by the Holy Spirit. Material blessing is always the bait in the hook and if that does not materialize in the life of the poor people there is the promise of heavenly life with golden crowns. Tithe is the basic income and references to it in the Bible are repeated without clarifying that it was meant for the landless Levites and the poor. Some churches and groups arrange a meal after the Sunday worship and they are normally the wealthy ones. The preachers know what are the biblical words, which will be attractive and alluring. As Paul says, the people also seek preachers of their own favour. But the story of exodus, prophetic messages on justice, compassion and equality, the parable of Good Samaritan, Jesus' criticism of false teachers, his appreciation for the extraordinary faith of some individuals from other faiths, the holistic liberation of the whole creation etc. are hardly touched by the fundamentalist preachers. Any critical questions they term as coming from worldly wisdom and unbelief.

Christian fundamentalism often triggers other fundamentalisms although their nature is different. For example, one may argue that the roots of Hindu fundamentalism lie in the exclusive Brahmanic belief in the inherent power of ritual and ideology of caste along with purity-pollution divide. The Islamic fundamentalism is based on the belief in immaculate revelation of the Qur'an and the infallible nature of its words. The extreme wings of fundamentalist Muslims think that the modern culture has lost its soul and killing those who subscribe to it qualify them to a quick transition to paradise. In all cases, there are dangerous dynamics of identities and vested interests. All fundamentalists share certain characteristics such as selection and literal interpretation of the favoured verses, claim for special place here and hereafter and conversion of others to their own religion or group. The various combinations and group dynamics have caused in India the current dangerous situation of politicization of religion and communalization of politics. The challenges of the

Hindutva movement, its political power and communal interest present a challenging situation, never before in the history of modern India. It calls Christians to prayerfully reread the Bible, re-imagine their identity, recapture the original vision of the evangelical faith, reconsider the content and methods of mission and evangelism. Understanding spirituality, reviewing the existing faith formulations, appreciating the ministry of interfaith dialogue, and revitalizing theological education at different levels become important.

It is impossible to provide detailed guidelines on all the issues of fundamentalism. However, what we provide below are not exhaustive yet hoped to be adequate to stimulate thinking and group discussion. The language is as simple as possible in a clear manner, but certain technical terms are not avoidable. It is our hope and prayer that the following guidelines will stir the mind of the readers that they will apply the insights to scriptural passages and concrete situations.

1. Understanding the Bible

1.1. The Bible is sacred and the basic guide for God's people. But it is not magical and therefore that even if a devil-possessed person refuses to receive it shows how superstitious is the devil! It is a unique book and a two-edged sword that requires very careful handling.

1.2. There is an accepted history of the origin and development of the Bible. That means, it did not fall from heaven as a finished product. It went through a long process of revelation in particular contexts, orally transmitted, handwritten on leather scrolls and papyrus grass, redacted, canonized, translated, printed and supplied.

1.3. Knowing the context of a book or a passage is important for understanding factual differences and perspectives. Take, for example, the difference between the books of Kings and Chronicles, three periods and authors with the name Isaiah, differing details of Jesus' birth in the Gospels of Matthew and Luke. Luke provides a key for gathering information and writing in his introduction: 'Many have undertaken to draw up an account of the things that have been fulfilled among us, just as they were handed down to us by those who from the first were eye witnesses and servants of the word. With this in mind, since I myself have carefully investigated everything from the beginning, I too decided to write an orderly account for you…' (Lk. 1: 1-3).

1.4. The Bible has more than one point of significance for Christians. Bible is a mark of Christian identity. At the same time we should respect the fact that nearly three-fourth of the Bible, the Hebrew scripture or the Old Testament, continues to be scripture of the Jews with a living tradition (Judaism). Centuries of anti-Jewish or anti-Semitic attitude has blinded Christians to take a proper view of what they call the Old Testament, which was the scripture of Jesus. It is true that the New Testament writers tried to present the happenings around Jesus were fulfilling the promises. But there are problems in trying to neatly connect them (e.g. 'the day of vengeance' in Is. 61: 2 is omitted in Lk. 4: 19).

1.5. Compared to scriptures of other religious traditions, the Christian scripture is very complex and complicated. It does not have the continuous flow of the instructions given by God nor poetic flow of devotion poured towards God. We should not expect ordinary Christians or outsiders will encounter always the love passages such as Jn. 3: 16 (God so loved the world…'). Without proper orientation they may be shocked by enigmatic myths, endless genealogies, ritual prescriptions, wars, drunkenness, butchery murders, romantic obsessions, sexual obscenity of famous leaders, tales of terror, and apocalyptic pictures of flashing images. By accepting such facts, we have a chance to be known as truth speaking people.

1.6. One important aspect of truth speaking is that we openly acknowledge that there are factual inconsistencies in the Bible. For example,

i. The word 'God' appears in Gen. 1: 1-2: 3 and then 'Lord God' throughout the second and third chapters and only 'Lord' in most of chapter four.

ii. According to Gen. 6: 20 God says that 'two' of every kind of bird, animal and creatures should enter the ark at the time of flood; but in 7: 2 God says, 'take seven pairs.'

iii. According to Jn. 1: 18 'no one has ever seen God,' but in Ex. 33: 11 we read that the Lord used to speak to Moses faces to face like a friend to a friend.

iv. According to 1 Sam. 15: 29 God does not change his mind as human beings do, but Jonah 3: 10 says that when the people of Nineveh turned from their evil ways God also changed his plan to destroy them.

v. When the Israelites asked for a king it grieved God as it amounted to rejecting his supremacy (1 Sam. 8: 6-7). But later God arranged for anointing Samuel, David and others who destroyed the original vision of the Jubilee and the ideal of simple leadership (see 1 Sam. 9, 16, 1 Kgs. 1).

vi. God instructed for various kinds of sacrifices as evident in the books of Exodus, Leviticus, Numbers and Deuteronomy. Later, there are references to positive notes on temple sacrifices (Is. 56: 7). But in many places, it is said that God never asked for any blood sacrifice but was pleased with thank-offerings and obedience (Ps. 50: 8-14; 51: 16; Is. 10: 15; 3: 23-24; 66: 3; Jer. 6: 20; 7: 21-23; Hos. 9: 4; Amos 5: 25).

vii. When king David proposed to build a temple for God, it was thwarted with the poignant note that when the Israelites were journeying in the wilderness God never asked for a dwelling place for himself but moved about their tents (2 Sa. 7: 6). Then immediately a contradicting note says that David's son will build a house for his Name (7: 13). Solomon built a temple with atrocious means and God accepted it with a condition (1 Kgs. 6-8).

viii. According to Matthew Jesus was born in Bethlehem, taken to Egypt, and fearing further danger, incidentally, brought to Nazareth in Galilee. The vision was to Joseph and visitors were the Magi (Mt. 1: 18-2: 23). But according to Luke, the family already lived in Nazareth and returned there. The original vision was to Mary. The birth of John the Baptist, Elizabeth-Mary meeting, Zechariah's song, decree of census, visit of shepherds, song of angels, the song of Simeon and the exclamation of Anna were additions in the narrative of

Luke. Interestingly Mark and John never bothered about the story of Jesus' birth.

ix. The anointing of Jesus just before his death is presented in varying details. Matthew writes that 'While Jesus was in Bethany in the home of Simon the Leper a woman came to him with an alabaster jar of very expensive perfume, which she poured on his head as he was reclining at the table' (26: 6-7). Mark writes the same (14: 3). Luke is silent. But for John it happened in Mary-Martha-Lazarus' house. Here it was Mary who poured the perfume on Jesus' feet and wiped his feet with her hair (Jn. 12: 18). The murmuring and Jesus' response also have difference.

x. The Passion narratives also differ. Most remarkably, Luke and John note three verses each of Jesus on the cross while Matthew and Mark note only one. Similarly, all the four Gospel writers differ in the detail, sequence and focus of the Easter experience.

1.7. The verses of 'promise and fulfillment' need to be understood carefully. In order to convince the Jews, the Gospel writers referred to their scripture that pointed to or foretold Jesus, the Messiah. But they are not always neat and relevant. We give three examples:

i. In the context of an imminent threat of war that shook the king and the people of Judah, God gave the sign of Immanuel ('God with us') in the form of a child born of a virgin or young woman (Is. 7: 14). In his dream the Lord appeared to Joseph, told about Mary's conception by the Holy Spirit, and said, 'She will give birth to a son, and you are to give him the name Jesus ('the Lord saves'), because he will save his people from their sins.' Subsequently, it is noted that this was to fulfill the above promise of Immanuel. Note the difference of names and meanings though they do not contradict.

ii. We read at every covenant service the following promise: In the coming days, declared the Lord, 'when I will make a new covenant with the people of Israel and with the people of Judah. It will not be like the covenant I made with their ancestors...they broke my covenant...This is the covenant I will make that...I will put my law in their minds and write it on their hearts...No longer they teach their neighbor, "Know the Lord," because they will all know me, from the least of them to the greatest' (Jer. 31: 31-34; cf. Is. 11: 9). After a period of six centuries, by his blood Jesus established by his own blood a 'new covenant' which was extended to cover his disciples and 'many' (Mt. 26: 28; Mk. 14: 24). Even after the number of disciples increased and churches established, there was misunderstanding and Paul, for example, had to exhort the Corinthian church (1Cori. 11: 17-34). The question is, when is the promise through Jeremiah was going to be fulfilled?

iii. According to Matthew, with the blood money thrown by the dejected Judas, the chief priests decided to use it to buy the potter's field as a burial place for foreigners. Matthew continues to state, 'what was spoken by Jeremiah the prophet was fulfilled: 'They took the thirty pieces of silver, the price set on him by the people of Israel, and they used them to buy the potter's field, as the Lord commanded me' (27: 7-10). Where is it recorded in the book of Jeremiah? In Jer. 19 we have a passing reference to a clay jar from a potter and breaking it to illustrate the condition of the people and their imminent destruction. And in 32: 7-9 we read of a purchase of a field at Anathoth by Jeremiah from his uncle for seventeen shekels. There is no resemblance with Matthew's reference. But in Zechariah 11: 12-13 in a completely different context there is mention of thirty pieces of silver, which were thrown to 'the potter at the house of the Lord.' Obviously, there is inaccurate and mistaken reference and there could be many reasons including twisting and faulty memory. These three examples of the problem of 'promise and fulfilment' provide us a key to understand all such connections. There is no doubt that there was genuine interest to communicate to the Jews that Jesus as Christ, prophet and Lord lived and taught according to the promises recorded in the Hebrew scripture.

Note: Acknowledging factual inconsistencies and faulty connections need not weaken the truth and undermine the meaning if they are rightly understood.

1.8. There is a danger of literal and allegorical interpretations. We are tempted to quote verses of our favour and draw literal meaning without any care about the context and later interpretation. For example,

i. We might insist the saving of a few and perishing of many with reference to what happened in Noah's time. But we should also point out God's eternal, cosmic and unconditional covenant that God would never destroy the earth by flood again. The rainbow was set on the cloud as a sign (Gen. 7-9). With reference to this story God spoke through prophet Isaiah saying that 'in a surge of anger I hid my face from you for a moment, but with everlasting kindness I will have compassion on you' (Is. 54: 54: f). Peter alleges that after resurrection, Jesus first went and proclaimed the gospel to the imprisoned 'spirits' in the time of flood (2 Pet. 3: 19-20). Now we get the full picture of God's attitude to the fallen humanity.

ii. There is always a temptation to focus on what is pleasing and beneficial for us but not taking the other side of our responsibilities. God called Abraham and told him 'I will bless you' and we interpret blessing as wealth, prosperity, health, security and so on. But God also told Abraham 'you will be a blessing' (Gen. 12: 1-3). What does it mean? We need to read the life and witness of Abraham which found expression in his giving priority to his nephew Lot, his refusal of booty offered by the king of Sodom and his insistence on payment for the burial cave for his wife. We can refer to other instances of blessing, particularly in the teaching of Jesus ('Blessed are those…').

iii. There are purity-pollution laws, blood sacrifice, polygamy, destruction of other nations, hostility to foreigners, cursing the enemies etc. If we read each text in the context, later correction and interpretation, then we will get a comprehensive picture and appeal to contemporary society and world. It is gravely misleading and dangerous too to apply the category of 'enemies' in the Bible to all sorts of those who are different to us or oppose us. What should be constantly ringing in our mind are commandments such as 'love the stranger' and 'love your enemies.'

iv. Allegorical interpretation is relatively scarce in the Bible. For example, Paul compares the slave woman Hagar to law given at mount Sinai and Sarah to freedom and promise (Gal. 4: 1-31). The context was the tendency of some Christians to revert to Judaism, persuaded by some teachers of the law. In 1 Cori.10: 1-4 he compares the Christian journey to the journey of Hebrew ancestors. 'They were all baptised into Moses in the cloud and in the sea. They all ate the same spiritual food and drank the same spiritual drink; for they drank from the spiritual rock that accompanied them, and that rock was Christ.' It is a radical interpretation with a view to persuade the Jews and Jewish Christians to believe that the Christ who manifested in Jesus was already present in the history of Israel. Similar perception is noted in Heb. 11: 25-26, which says that Moses preferred to suffering with his people to enjoying the pleasure in Pharo's palace, 'for the sake of Christ.' All such comparisons are different from the popular Christian allegorical interpretation of slavery to Egypt is slavery to sin, salvation is through the blood of a lamb (Jesus), journey in the wilderness as life of trials and tribulations, Jordan as death and Canaan as the paradise of joy. One more example could be the interpretation of the parable of Good Samaritan given through centuries of Christian history. Accordingly, the traveler from Jerusalem to Jericho is the sinner, robbers who left him half dead are the devil and his hosts, the passers-by priest and Levite of the Old Testament religion, the good Samaritan is Jesus who descended from heaven, oil is the Spirit, the inn is the church, and two coins are two Testaments or two sacraments and his coming again is Jesus' second coming. In this spurious interpretation Jesus' teaching to be a good neighbor to the needy is completely lost!

v. It is obvious that the only most basic commandment is what Jesus termed as the greatest: 'Love the Lord your God with all your heart and with all your soul and with all your mind and with all your strength; and love the neighbor as yourself (Mk. 12: 30-31). It is most comprehensive covering passion, feeling, knowledge, action and living for others. It may take one life time to realise fully the demands of this commandment, but neglecting it would make all our reading of the Bible futile.

1.9. The message of a book or text is not always obvious and clear and the reader may have to decipher the spirit and content depending on the context. Take the book of Job for example. First, in response to Job's questions about his suffering and God's justice, his friends present many solutions. They appear to be plausible and even fascinating. But at the end God is angry with them and Job is performing a sacrifice for their atonement. God says that they did not speak as his servant Job. What does it mean? What is the solution of the book for human suffering? Why should Job sit in ashes for speaking? Does God shut up Job? There is no direct answer and an engaging reading of the dialogue of the book may help us to raise right questions about suffering and not straight answers.

1.10. Jesus' approach to the scripture: Jesus was a devout Jew and engaging reader of his scripture, raising questions and applying the message to the local context. We can identify four principles that governed Jesus' approach to the scripture as evident in the Synoptic Gospels. They are rejection, reflection, revision and selection.

i. Jesus rejects two kinds of approach to the scripture. One is the literalist approach as represented by the devil at the time of his temptation in the wildness. The other is the minutely detailed explanation of the law by Pharisees and Scribes emphasizing the trivial things but ignoring the weightier matters.

   After reading Jesus' approach, one may say that a literalist approach to particular text of the scripture is satanic. The story of Jesus' temptation by the devil makes the point clear. Even scripture is a tool in the hand of Satan to tempt religious people! 'Then the devil took him to the holy city, and set him on the parapet of the temple. 'If you are the Son of God', he said, 'throw yourself down; for scripture says, "He will give his angels in charge of you, and they will support you in their arms, for fear you should strike your foot against a stone." Jesus answered him, 'Scripture also says, "You are not to put the Lord your God to the test" (Mt. 4: 5-7; also, see Lk. 4: 9-12).

   The devil is quoting Ps. 91: 11,12. Jesus is countering this way of seeking a literalist meaning by quoting Deut. 6: 16. In the other two temptations also, Jesus counters the argument by quoting Deut. 8:3 ('not by bread alone') and Deut. 6:13 ('Serve your Lord God alone'). What the devil had quoted in these temptations is not mentioned. It is reasonable, however, to infer that the devil might have pointed out the food miraculously brought by God for the Israelites in the wilderness when he asked Jesus to command stones to become bread. Likewise, he might have pointed out verses, which promise power and authority for those who sought

God's help when he asked Jesus to bow down before him. In any case Jesus' counter-quotations are very appropriate.

The Pharisees and Scribes interpreted the laws very minutely with complex ramifications. But Jesus says, 'Alas for you, scribes and Pharisees, hypocrites! You pay tithes of mint and dill and cumin; but you have overlooked the weightier demands of the law - justice, mercy, and good faith. It is these you should have practised, without neglecting the others. Blind guides! You strain off a midge, yet gulp down a camel!' (Mt. 23: 23, 24).

The spirit of the Pharisees and Scribes seems to haunt the minds of many Christians today when they debate for hours on the right form of baptism etc. without taking the weightier matters of new life, justice and liberation seriously. Or they may discuss the implications of the last judgment for Hindus and Muslims without taking seriously the imperative to love them.

Elsewhere Jesus points out how the readers of the scriptures can miss the central point of their witness. 'You study the scriptures diligently, supposing that in having them you have eternal life; their testimony points to me, yet you refuse to come to me to receive that life' (Jn. 5: 39, 40).

Even after years of reading and searching the Bible one may not come to have a grip of this fundamental witness. Therefore, reading the Bible without a proper perspective is rejected by Jesus as much as he rejected the literalist approach.

ii. Jesus said, 'Do not suppose that I have come to abolish the law and the prophets; I did not come to abolish, but to complete. Truly I tell you: so long as heaven and earth endure, not a letter, not a dot, will disappear from the law until all that must happen has happened' (Mt. 5: 17, 18).

By these words, what does Jesus tell us? Does he claim that he has observed all the minute rules of the law known in his tradition? If so, why was he accused of revolting against the tradition? Presumably, the Scribes and Pharisees considered the law to be perfect as it was God's revelation and observance of all the rules literally would bring them merit. Jesus is also concerned even about the 'least of the law's demands' (Mt. 5:19). But for him the law was given with a view to proceeding toward perfection. Therefore, a spirit of loving submission to God through its observance was important for him. That is why he told his disciples, 'unless you show yourselves far better than the scribes and Pharisees, you can never enter the kingdom of Heaven' (Mt. 5: 20).

In the process of growing into greater righteousness towards the perfection of God a constant revision of the laws becomes imperative. At first sight they may look impossible ideals. But those who fix their mind on the heavenly Father who is perfect, will, with perfect freedom and joy, try to follow them. Matthew records six examples of Jesus revising the prevalent moral codes of the law as prescribed and explained by the Rabbis.

(a) It was said, 'Do not commit murder; anyone who commits murder must be brought to justice.' But Jesus said: 'Anyone who nurses anger against his brother must be brought to justice.' Jesus seems to mean that anger is the passion that impels murder, which is as offensive as murder itself. To say to one's brother 'good for nothing' deserves the sentence of the court; whoever calls him 'fool' deserves hell fire.'. Hence, the importance of being reconciled with one's brother in good time (5: 21-26).

(b) Similarly, a lustful gaze is equal to committing adultery (5: 27-30).

(c) Divorce was easily allowed on flimsy grounds (burning out food and talking loudly). But for Jesus 'if a man divorces his wife for any cause other than un-chastity, he involves her in adultery' (5: 31, 32).

(d) Since swearing cannot make one hair white or black it should be replaced by a plain 'Yes' or 'No' (5: 33-37).

(e) The practice of 'an eye for an eye and a tooth for a tooth' was a developed moral code in Israel as the practice around was taking several eyes for one eye and so on. But even then, if 'an eye for an eye and a tooth for a tooth' (5:38) is strictly practised, the majority of the people in this world will be blind and toothless. Realising this problem, Jesus said that, 'if anyone slaps you on the right cheek, turn and offer him the other also' (5: 39).

(f) Instead of 'You have heard that it was said, "Love your neighbour and hate your enemy." But I tell you…' - the first part of the injunction is found in Lev. 19: 18, but 'as yourself' is omitted. But the second part ('hate your enemy') is non-biblical!

In any case, for Jesus, instead of hating one's enemy one should love them thereby become the child of the heavenly Father (5: 43-45).

The conclusion of revising the law is interesting. Why should one love his/her enemy? In what way is the Heavenly Father's goodness is boundless? God, the heavenly Father, 'causes the sun to rise on good and bad alike, and sends the rain on the innocent and the wicked' (5: 45). This note provides a criterion for any revision of scriptural instructions. The revision is valid if it takes us towards the perfection of God, which is demonstrated in his regular gifts for humanity irrespective of their moral standard. Paul reflects this supreme idea when he prays for the Ephesians that they 'may be filled with the very fullness of God' (Eph. 3:19).

1.11. We have already seen how Jesus was selective in making connections with scriptural verses. His deliberate choice of a particular tradition or story is clearer in the following examples.

i. Priests, Pharisees and Scribes pointed out stories, which legitimised priestly authority with a notion of sacredness attached to particular places and articles. Even today there are priests and preachers who threaten those who question them. They refer to the stories like Korah and his group who questioned the overbearing behaviour of Moses and Aaron, for which they were destroyed by God (Num. 16). They are happy about what happened to Uzzah when he put out his hand innocently with good intention to the ark of God and took hold of it as the oxen carrying the cart stumbled. God smote him (2 Sam. 6: 6, 7). Naturally the ordinary laity will be terrified by such stories. But Jesus never quoted such stories but the contrary ones. For instance, when the Pharisees criticised his disciples for plucking heads of grain and eating on a Sabbath day, Jesus responded saying, 'Have you not read what David did, when he and his men were hungry? He went into the house of God and ate the sacred bread, though neither he nor his men had a right to eat it, but only the priests. Or have you not read in the law that on the Sabbath the priests in the temple break the Sabbath and they are not held to be guilty? But I tell you, there is something greater than the temple here. If you had known what this text means, 'It is mercy I require, not sacrifice', you would not have condemned the innocent' (Mt. 12: 3-7; Cf.1 Sam. 21: 2-7).

   Mark and Luke also mention this incident (Mk. 2:23-27; Lk. 6:3,4). This incident tells us that when we quote the past traditions for justifying our present actions we must pick up only those reflecting progressive views.

ii. Jesus referred to the creation stories when a question on divorce was raised (Mt. 19: 3-9). Watch carefully how he differs from Paul in this regard. Jesus holds that for the hardness of men's hearts Moses allowed them to divorce their wives (otherwise, their life would have been miserable in their husbands' homes). But from the beginning it was

> not so. He refers to the first creation story, which says that in the beginning God created human beings male and female (Gen. 1: 26). But Paul was swinging between the conservative Jewish idea on women and the liberative Christian idea on them. When he exhorted women to 'learn, listening quietly and with due submission' and 'not to teach or dictate to the men' he refers to the second story of creation found in the second chapter of the book of Genesis and to the story of the Fall in the third chapter. Accordingly, Paul tells us, 'Adam was created first, Eve afterwards; moreover it was not Adam who was deceived; it was the woman who, yielding to deception, fell into sin' (1 Tim. 2: 1-14). Equally interesting is that in the same context Jesus refers to a particular verse from the second creation story: 'That is why a man leaves his father and mother and is united to his wife, and the two become one flesh' (Mt. 19: 5). But in a different context, Paul connects the words 'two shall become one flesh' with the relationship of a man with a prostitute (1 Cor. 6: 16) although in Eph. 5: 31 the connection is positive. Today the test before us is whether to select Jesus or Paul in this matter. Everyone, including the fundamentalists, is selective in dealing with the scripture. But the question is on what basis (or even bias) do we select!

1.12. Reflection includes having an overall perspective and making right connections when one approaches the scripture. On the way to Emmaus, the risen Jesus accompanied his disciples but they did not recognise him when they shared with him the death of Jesus and the experience of those who had found an empty tomb and heard the angels saying that he was alive. Jesus chided them for their slow-heartedness to believe all that the prophets had spoken. He also pointed out the necessity of the Christ to suffer and then enter into his glory. More revealingly, it is stated, 'Then, starting from Moses and all the prophets, he explained to them in the whole of scripture the things that refer to himself' (Lk. 24: 27). Later on, when the disciples' eyes were opened and they recognised him and Jesus vanished out of their sight they said to each other: 'Were not our hearts on fire as he talked with us on the road and explained the scriptures to us' (24: 32)?

What does interpreting or opening the scriptures here mean? Did Jesus explain to them verse by verse all that Moses and the prophets had said within a short time? Obviously not. Rather, presumably, he pointed out the central axis of God's dealing with humanity, that is, death and resurrection. The cross and resurrection of Jesus was not simply the one time experience of an individual, but it reflected the suffering and glory of God which was shared by Moses and by prophets like Jeremiah in their own life.

In this reflective model of interpreting the scripture a careful way of connecting verses and events is important. This is in no way identical with the way the Gospel writers connected things. In order to convince the Jews they tried to present all that happened in the life of Jesus as fulfilling the prophecies of the Hebrew scripture. The problems of such connecting has been pointed out above.

Jesus' making references to the Hebrew scriptural verses does not bear the mark of the 'letter' but the 'spirit', which is a basic feature in his reflection on the scripture. For example, in response to the Sadducees who ridiculed the belief in resurrection, Jesus does not quote Job or some inter-testament books where there are glimpses of the idea of bodily resurrection. He first retorted saying 'How far you are from the truth! You know neither the scriptures nor the power of God' (Mt. 22: 29). Then, according to Luke, he points to Moses and the burning bush 'where he calls the Lord ("I am") the God of Abraham and the God of Isaac and the God of Jacob'. And Jesus adds, 'God is not God of the dead but of the living; in his sight all are alive' (Lk. 20: 37, 38; Mt. 23: 32f; Mk. 12: 26). It is implicit that the burning bush itself was a sign of hope or resurrection. It was burning, symbolising the groaning of people and the burning heart of God but was not consumed. It provides a key to understanding history, peoples' suffering and hope. This way of making connection with past events attracted some scribes who said, 'Well spoken, Teacher' (Lk. 20: 39).

At the time of Jesus' triumphal entry into Jerusalem surrounded by the poor masses, children cried out in the temple saying, 'Hosanna to the son of David.' But the chief priests were indignant and they said to him. 'Do you hear what these are saying?' And Jesus said to them, 'I do. Have you never read the text, 'You have made children and babes at the breast sound your praise aloud?"' (Mt. 21: 16). Obviously here Jesus refers to Ps. 8: 2. But the second part of this verse, omitted by Matthew, brings out the whole purport of Jesus recalling it, that is, 'to restrain the enemy and the avenger.' The babes signify the weak and by praising their Lord they challenge the powerful. According to Luke it was 'the whole company of his disciples' who praised God with a loud voice (Lk. 19: 37). Similarly in the subsequent event of cleansing the temple Jesus appropriately refers to Isa. 56: 7 and Jer. 7: 11 together: 'Does not scripture say, "My house shall be called a house of prayer for all nations?" But you have made it a robbers' cave' (Mk. 11: 17; Mt. 21: 13 and Lk. 19: 46 omits 'for all nations'). This way of referring to the scripture stands consistent with Jesus' critical attitude to his own religion and its structures (read Mt. 13: 14; Mk. 4: 12; cf. Is. 6: 9, 10).

Let us see one more example. Following the parable of the wicked tenants, Jesus said to the chief priests and elders of the people: 'The stone, which the builders rejected has become the main corner stone. This is the Lord's doing, and it is wonderful in our eyes?' (Mt. 21: 42; Mk. 12: 10; Ps. 118: 22, 23).

Jesus alludes to his rejection by his own religious community. He understands his own suffering in the light of the 'suffering servant' spoken by Isaiah and lived out by Jeremiah. Unlike the 'fulfilment formula' of the Gospel writers, he took the overall pattern of God's dealing with humanity the aspects of which are mentioned at random in the Bible. He could pick up the correct connections, as they were rightly applicable to his life, its struggles and its purpose. Even his last cry on the cross 'my God, my God why have you forsaken me' was taken from the scripture (Ps. 22: 1) but relevantly. Those who reflect on the scripture in relation to their actual involvement in a ministry of struggle and liberation are able to put their finger on the right verses, but not those who open the Bible blindly.

The four principles adopted by Jesus in his approach to the scripture is applicable to all those who take the scripture seriously. While the early Christians extolled the divine origin of prophesy and sacred writing, there is no evidence that they followed these principles. However, as we have already pointed out earlier, they did recognise the need of interpretation and the possibility of the wavering and uneducated for twisting and misunderstanding the scriptural texts (2 Pet. 3: 15-16). For Paul, 'Everything that was written in the past was written to teach us, so that through the endurance taught in the Scriptures and the encouragement they provide we might have hope' (Rom. 15: 4). Today Christians have greater responsibility than Jesus and the apostles, because they have a new section called New Testament added to their scriptures, and this addition was made much later than the time of Jesus. As affirmed by one New Testament writer, 'The word of God is alive and active. It cuts more keenly than any two-edged sword, piercing so deeply that it divides soul and spirit, joints and marrow; it discriminates among the purposes and thoughts of the heart' (Heb. 4: 12). Needless to say, how much care needs to be taken in handling such a sword!

1.13. The historical context of a book or text needs to be taken seriously. Otherwise we will miss the message or may be confused about it. One difficulty is that the sixty six books (Protestant) of the Bible are not ordered historically. It should be a separate study to understand the origin, redaction, selection and chronological order of the books. One striking example could be that the book of Ruth which approved interreligious marriage should have been placed just after Ezra and Nehemiah where there was a crisis when the exiles returned to Jerusalem with their foreign wives. The book of Isaiah contains at least three books (1-39, 40-55, 56-66) and the opening verses of each book give clues for the historic period and context.

Similarly, if there is a possibility to record the books historically readers will find it easier to grasp the message. Otherwise, the guidance of those who have proper training to handle the scripture becomes indispensable.

1.14. It is often criticised, mainly by Jews, that Christians pollute their pulpits by certain stereotypes about them. For example, did Jesus condemn all the Jews? Were all the Jews responsible for the death of Jesus? Were those who shouted 'Hosanna' (Galilean masses) during the triumphal entry of Jesus the same as who shouted 'crucify him' (those Jewish leaders who had access to Pilate's place)? Anti-Jewish animosity and atrocity of Christians for many centuries are like raw wounds in the memory of well-meaning Jews.

1.15. Symbolic meaning of entities like blood will prevent the communication of the gospel of God's love. Blood sacrifice in the Bible was gradually losing its significance. As we pointed out earlier, a prophetic tradition denied the divine institution of blood sacrifice in the first place. In Hos. 6: 6 we read, 'For I desire mercy, not sacrifice and acknowledgement of God rather than burnt offerings.' Jesus quoted this twice (Mt. 9: 13; 12: 7). However, the symbolism of 'blood' continued in the church. When Jesus asked his hearers to eat his flesh and drink his blood, some Jews found it disgusting and some of his disciples left him (Jn. 6). In few places in the New Testament the cross was interpreted as shedding the atoning blood for sins (1Tim. 2: 6; 1Pet. 1: 19; 1Jn. 1: 9; 2: 1-2). The writer to the Hebrews gives an exposition in which he depicts Jesus as the greatest High Priest and supreme sacrifice, thus bringing the institution of blood sacrifice to an end. In any case, it is one of the many interpretations. Literal interpretations of Jesus' blood as atoning to God for human sin have created great confusion and misunderstanding in the Church. In missionary preaching we have several instances of explaining the blood as symbol of life-giving and God's suffering heart and his sharing people's pain. Therefore, devotional expressions such as 'washing in the blood' and 'he shed blood for my sins' will distort the central focus of gospel of the suffering love of God.

1.16. Personal Caricature: Traditionally, we have categorized some persons good and guided by God and some others bad and demonic. Here too we have to follow the attitude of Jesus. Sometimes what the writers write can be prejudiced. Here we illustrate with three persons, two projected as good and one bad.

i. David is considered as a great hero, king, master builder and pious poet. But the narratives of his life-style and achievements raise number of questions. For example, why did he forget his low estate of a remote hamlet Bethlehem? Can we justify his bloodshed? His sex life was a scandal and did not hesitate to take additional wives by killing their husbands. Can it be a model for a ruler? His urbanization alienated the poor people and his legacy proved that kingship was not God's liking in the first place. Now it is an accepted fact that there have been ghost writers for famous kings. Those who hold David in high esteem may be shocked by these remarks?

   Let us start with Jesus' remarks about David. Once he presented a riddle about David to a group of Pharisees. When David himself has said the Messiah being his Lord sitting at his right hand, how can be the Son of David? (Mt. 22: 41-46; cf. Mk. 12: 35-37a; Lk. 20: 41-44). Nobody dared to answer and ask further questions!

   The Hebrew text of Psalm 110 and the meaning are a moot question. However, if the context is inferred correctly and the singer is clarified there is no insurmounting problem. Most of the English translations attribute the psalm to David. There is a difference of opinion about the title. The REB puts it: 'For David: a psalm' and verse 1 is translated as follows: 'This is the LORD's oracle to my lord: 'Sit at my right hand, and I shall make your enemies your footstool.'

   The Greek and most English versions of Psalm 110: 1 quoted by Jesus come from the Greek translation (LXX) of the Hebrew Bible. Jesus takes the text in its ambiguity.

Jesus' question assumes several rabbinical views including that David was inspired by the divine spirit, was its author, and that *adoni* designated the Messiah. Did Jesus ask an unanswerable question? The question obviously implies no claim of his own to the title of Messiah and Son of David. One can discern here the implicit preference of Jesus (or Matthew) for 'Son of God' to 'son of David.' It is farfetched to think that the purpose of Jesus asking this question was to point out the inadequate knowledge of the Pharisees about the textual difficulties in certain parts of the Hebrew scripture or about the rabbinic literature.

It is more reasonable to think that, using the ambiguity of a text, Jesus was implicitly arguing that though he could be perceived to be the Messiah, the title 'Son of David' should not lead people to think that he was going to restore, unite and rule the united kingdom of Israel by the methods and style applied by David whose reign was considered to represent the golden period in their past history. To go a step further, Jesus was doing a silent revolution subverting the legacy of David. David represented an epic hero with ingenious and manipulative power who deviated the original vision of a simple leader (as embodied by the first king Saul) tainting his throne and crown with blood of the innocent people and unlimited number of wives and concubines.

The immediate son of David (Solomon) led this tyranny to a climax that proved to be a havoc in the history of the 'people of God.' But the uncritical glorification of David (and Solomon) in the Christian tradition has been due to the piety and poetic achievement with a charismatic charm attributed to them without questioning their authenticity in the context of a tyranny which demanded uncritical submission.

In the New Testament, with a view to convince the Jews, the Gospel writers present Jesus as the 'Son of David' (Mt. 1: 1, 20; cf. Lk. 1: 27). Particularly, Mark writes that during Jesus' triumphal entry into Jerusalem, the crowd exclaimed, 'Blessed is the kingdom of our father David that is coming! Hosanna in the heavens" (Mk. 11: 10). However, the idea that Jesus reversed David's corrupt legacy has found expression in certain specific areas. The contrast between David and Jesus is clear in their basic identifications of life and work as evident in three areas.

Geographically, Luke calls Bethlehem as the city ('little town') of David (Lk. 2: 5,10). David came from Bethlehem, which was then a remote village with a shepherd community (1 Sam. 16:4). Instead of the technological armor, he was more comfortable with his staff and smooth stones when he confronted Goliath (17: 38-40). David was made king in Hebron, a semi-urban town (2 Sam. 5: 1-5). Soon after this he captured Jerusalem conquering the Jebusites and named it 'the City of David' (5: 9). Later it was celebrated as the 'city of God' because of the temple built there (Ps. 48: 1,8; 87: 3). Jerusalem grew in great popularity and the Zionists of the time expected that people of all nations would go there and that the word of the Lord would come from there (Is. 2: 2-3; Mic. 4: 2). The centrality of Jerusalem was also part of the increasing urbanization, and planning house of commerce and war. Some prophets were so critical as to wish its destruction (Jer. 7: 29, 13: 9, 26: 18; Mic. 3: 12). Toward the end of his life David longed to have a drink of water from the well by the gate of Bethlehem and three heroic men made it possible but then he refused to drink as he saw it the blood of those men (2 Sam. 23: 15-17). However, it was too late to return to his village.

The 'rural prophet' Micah revived the memory of Bethlehem by announcing that the Messiah would come from there (Mic. 5: 2). This was recalled when Jesus was born and Bethlehem was near enough to perturb Herod and all the people of Jerusalem (Mt. 2: 1-6). According to Matthew, after fleeing massacre of male babies and taking refuge in

Egypt and sensing further trouble in Judea, Jesus' family went to Galilee and settled down in a town called Nazareth (Mt. 2: 22f). Jesus fully identified with himself with the local peasant community and was called Nazarene. Nazareth in Jesus' time was so backward as to make Nathanael exclaim 'can anything good come from Nazareth?' (Jn. 1:46). John also notes that there was a dispute about the place of the Messiah – somewhere in Galilee or Bethlehem? (Jn. 7: 41-43). Jesus did most of his ministry in Galilee and went to Jerusalem to confront the religious authority and to weep over it (Lk. 19: 41). People acclaimed him, 'This is the prophet Jesus, from Nazareth in Galilee' (Mt. 21: 11). Jesus was arrested and executed in Jerusalem but the Risen Lord went to Galilee! Relatedly, for Matthew, the Great Commission was given not from Jerusalem but from a mountain in Galilee (Mt. 28: 16).

ii. Ministerially, after cleansing the temple, Matthew notes, 'In the temple the blind and the crippled came to (Jesus), and he healed them' (21: 14). To appreciate the significance of this event we should know the greatest massacre of the handicapped (David said his 'bitter enemies') at the behest of David when he captured the city of the Jebusites and the tradition that accrued from it was that 'No one who is blind or lame is to come into the Lord's house' (2 Sam. 5: 8). It is no wonder that the chronicler omitted this horrible event when he recorded the story (1 Chr. 11: 4-9). It left the legacy that in Jesus' time the blind and the lame were kept outside the temple and Jesus initiated a 'triumphal entry' of the handicapped into the temple by inviting them in and healing them.

Apart from the above exclamation at his 'triumphal entry' there were two kinds of people who used the title 'Son of David' for addressing Jesus: the handicapped and the Gentiles, both were the enemies of David. The two blind men and another blind man, Bartimaes, would illustrate the first category (Mt. 9: 27-30; 20: 30-34; Mk. 10: 47-52; Lk. 18: 35-43). Relatedly, when Jesus healed a blind and dumb demoniac all the bystanders were amazed, and the word went around: 'Can this be the Son of David?' The second category could be illustrated by a Canaanite woman calling Jesus 'Son of David' when she approached Jesus for the healing of her daughter who had been possessed by a demon. Though Jesus first told her the limitation of his ministry, after seeing her persistence to broaden his boundary to cover the Gentiles, he appreciated her 'faith' and healed her daughter (Mt. 15: 21-28).

iii. Administratively, when David was a fugitive, apart from his brothers and all his family, 'Everyone in any kind of distress or in debt or with a grievance gathered round him, about four hundred in number, and he became their chief' (1 Sam. 22: 2). The number soon increased to six hundred (30: 9). As a king, his administrative council consisted of the army chief, secretary of state, adjutant-general, commanders of regional guards, priests (2 Sam. 8: 15-18), mighty fighters, servants and soldiers and heroes (2 Sam. 10: 7; 16: 6; 17: 8; 20: 7; 23: 8-38). After his victory over the Philistines, when David entered Jerusalem with the Ark, he was leaping and whirling before the Lord surrounded by musicians and slave-girls (6: 12ff). Compare this with the 'Son of David', who at the time of his triumphal entry was surrounded by multitude of disciples or Galilean masses including the children (Mt. 21: 16; Lk. 19: 37). When the priests and scribes were indignant at the boys' shout in the temple with the words 'Son of David', Jesus quoted Ps. 8: 2 saying 'You have made children and babes at the breast sound your praise aloud.' This was the way he had chosen 'to restrain the enemy and the avenger.' In Jesus' teaching children and babes were the symbolic representations of the vulnerable, powerless yet powerful in love and trust, thus qualified to enter the kingdom of God. That was well in tune with the expectation of the Messianic age in the Hebrew scripture: 'Then the wolf will live with the lamb, and the leopard lie down with the kid; the calf and the young lion will feed together, with a little child to tend them...The infant will play over the cobra's hole, and the young child dance over the viper's nest' (Is. 11: 6-8).

It is significant to note that, when David forgot his origin and followed the ethos of some neighboring kings being autocratic and excessive self-indulgence, prophet Isaiah imagines the new image of the Messiah with the opening words 'a shoot will come up from the stump of Jesse' (11: 1). This was to go back to the simple origins of David. But the kings of Israel and Judah could not turn the tables around and with the exile it was gloom and doom. Most radically, the Persian ruler, Cyrus, was projected as the Messiah, the anointed, and he, though a foreigner and worshipper of his own deities, came to epitomize the aspirations of people, freedom and prosperity. Thus, in the prophetic revelation and imagination the Davidic lineage was broken and this created greater confusion and greater number of opinions of who the true Messiah was.

However, the Davidic lineage of Jesus was affirmed in the preaching of the early apostles (Acts 2: 25-28, 34, 35; cf. 13: 22, 34; 15: 16; Romans 1: 3: 2 Tim. 2: 8; 4: 25-27). Paul quotes David with reference to verses from psalms in support of the gospel he preached (Rom. 4: 6; 11:9). But there is no critical evaluation of David's rule and contrasting to that of Jesus.

When Jesus' overt struggle with powers and authorities was revived at the time of persecution from Rome, the early Christians revived the 'riddle' and in a style of 'political cartoon' they presented Jesus in contrast to David but holding the mysterious key of a complex and complicated history of the world dominated by tyrannies. This picture, which combines the Jewish vision is presented fascinatingly in the last book of the Bible. Thus, Jesus is introduced: 'These are the words of the Holy One, the True One, who had David's key, so that when he opens the door, no one can shut it, and when he shuts it, no one can open it' (Rev. 3: 7). When no one responded to a divine call to come forward and open the seal of a mysterious scroll (the scroll of human life!) John who saw this vision in his open prison wept bitterly. Then one of the elders told him not to weep for 'the Lion from the tribe of Juda, the shoot growing from David's stock, has won the right to open the scroll and its seven seals.' Then John saw a Lamb with the marks of sacrifice on him, who had seven horns and seven eyes which are the seven spirits of God sent to every part of the world. The Lamb came and received the scroll from the right hand of the One who sat on the throne (5: 5-7). This is the greatest picture of an enigmatic power, crucified yet surviving. Jesus says towards the end of the last book: 'I am the offspring of David, the shoot growing from his stock, the bright star of dawn' (22: 16). But the Christian rulers and administrators of the Churches forgot the original vision of the 'root of Jesse' and the image of Lion-turned-Lamb which signify the power of powerlessness. Perhaps the popular choice of the name for male babies in the Christian world based not on this meaning but the meaning of David the king, a mighty hero, shrewd politician, murderous for romance and who united the kingdom.

iv. In the case of Solomon, who carried a scandal at his birth which was removed by God's special naming him as 'beloved', his celebrated wisdom drifted to the extreme of craftiness from the beginning and many innocent ones were finished off. We need to read 1Kgs. 1-11 at the stretch to have a clear picture of this drift which developed into most horrible ends. Briefly, Adonijah, Solomon's older half-brother, the heir-presumptive to David's throne was sidelined by Bathsheba who had succeeded in her conspiracy to make her wily son the king. He had asked Solomon to give him Abishag, a young concubine of David, as his wife. Just making use of this request, Adonijah was struck down to death. Also, Solomon removed the illustrious Abiathar from priesthood. Joab, the famous captain who had conspired with Adonijah, was chased and he took refuge at the altar of the tent holding the horns. When he refused to come out, throwing away all the norms of a sacred place, on Solomon's order he was killed there itself. Shimei, a kinsman of Saul, who once shouted to David saying 'you man of blood, you scoundrel' (2 Sam.16: 7), was killed with a silly excuse. After narrating these series of killing, some instigated by David and others on Solomon's own will, the book of 2 Kings, chapter 2 ends with the statement, 'The kingdom was now firmly established in Solomon's hands.' Thus, there were no more contenders or opponents! Worst of all, the name of the Lord was taken in his favour and more glaringly in the following course of events.

Solomon's temple project was shrouded with unjust and deceptive practices. He had an agreement with Hiram the king of Tyre for timber, training in skills and gold, but the latter was terribly disappointed by the twenty (barren) villages Solomon gave in Galilee (5: 1-12; 9: 10-14). Solomon conscripted at his will thousands of laborers and skilled workers from all Israel (5: 13-18). Forced labour was introduced for the first time in Israel. The tax was too heavy about which no one could open his/her mouth and all these were openly expressed after the death of Solomon. Anyway, the magnificent temple was dedicated in pomp and celebration. Solomon's dedicatory prayer has the element of showing himself as a faithful king (8: 22-61), but God said very clearly that he could not be domesticated in the temple and would not tolerate injustice. Nothing could be taken for granted and if Solomon and his successors did not walk before God in integrity of heart and uprightness, God would reject the temple which will then become a byword and an object of ridicule among peoples (9: 1-9).

In his craftiness in the garb of wisdom Solomon married hundreds of foreign wives through peace agreement of convenience and it left a legacy of warning against interfaith marriage (Neh. 13: 26). While maintenance of a colony of women was a great burden on the economy, the foreign wives turned Solomon's heart after other gods, tragically, the Lord became angry with the 'wise and pious' son of David, and raised adversaries against Solomon (11: 1-18). After his ruthless reign the united kingdom of Israel was divided causing untold conflicts and suffering. Jesus, a different son of David, was intelligent and innocent, but ridiculed the tradition of Solomon's wisdom and glory when he said that not even Solomon in all his splendor was dressed like the lilies of the field (Mt. 6: 28f). He rightfully claimed to be greater than Solomon (12: 42).

There are proverbs ascribed to Solomon and there are reasons to question his authorship of many of them. In any case, what is said in 'his' proverbs is not practiced in his life and kingly rule. Solomon played the greatest havoc in the history of Israel. He and his father David are more a warning than models for today.

v. Judas, one of the disciples of Jesus, is normally caricatured as robber, greedy and traitor. But behind the popular narratives of the Gospel writers we see a man who was peculiar but true searcher after truth. Judas expressed some genuine concern about the extravagant acts (Mary's anointing of Jesus with perfume) while there were poor people around, but it was construed as showing his greedy nature. This was connected with the fact that he was carrying the common purse (Jn. 12: 3ff). In Jn. 13: 18 Jesus alleges the odd one among his chosen ones with making a reference to Ps. 41: 9: 'he who eats bread with me has turned against me.' Obviously here the Psalmist alludes to his close friend turning against at times of crisis. Jesus' early dialogue with Judas in connection with betrayal and calling him friend at the time of betrayal and arrest (Mt. 26: 25, 47-50) does not overtly suggest a condemnation from him. Calling him a devil might not be as serious as one would normally think, because such titles were casually used in conversation between rabbis. Peter too was rebuked with the word Satan (Mt. 16: 23)!

A key problem in the four Gospels is the ability to understand the nature and function of the kingdom of God on earth, 'among yourselves.' The disciples continue to misunderstand its nature and the promise of a ruling role for all the twelve. They always fought for the highest position, the position of being seated on the left and right hand sides of Jesus. Jesus' teaching on becoming humble like a child, the highest being the lowest, not to be served but to serve, did not make a dent in their consciousness. Where Jesus was rejected they wanted to call down fire from heaven and consume the people of that place (Lk. 9: 54). They did not suppose that if he wanted Jesus could appeal for help at times of crisis from his Father who at once would send 'more than twelve legions of angels' (Mt. 26: 53). Then, their question was as to why Jesus continued to be tolerant and passive. To Jesus' great frustration, just before he ascended into heaven, when he spoke of the baptism with the Holy Spirit, the disciples asked him, 'Lord, is this the time at which you are to restore sovereignty to Israel?' Jesus answered, 'It is not for you to know about dates or times which the Father has set in his own control. But you...will bear witness to me...even in the farthest corners of the earth' (Acts 1: 6-8). If Jesus was an ordinary leader of a movement with such dull-headed, slow-thinking-understanding band of disciples, it may not be unreasonable to imagine terrible disappointment and frustration.

It is in the light of the above context we can see the attitude and suicidal act of Judas. Without forgetting what we have noted earlier about the possible intimate friendship of Judas with Jesus and his concern about the poor, let us carefully read a few clues that appear in the Fourth Gospel in a peculiar way. It was before the Passover festival, at the last supper, the devil had already put it into the mind of Judas to betray him. During supper, Jesus well aware that the Father had entrusted everything to him, and that he had come from God and was going back to God, rose from the supper table, took off his outer garment and, taking a towel, tied it round him. Then he poured water into a basin, and began to wash his disciples' feet and to wipe with the towel. Jesus exclaimed in deep distress, 'In very truth I tell you, one of you is going to betray me.' That disciple who leaned back close to Jesus and asked, 'Lord who is it?' Jesus replied, 'It is the one to whom I give this piece of bread when I have dipped it in the dish.' Then he took it, dipped it in the dish, and gave it to Judas, son of Simon Iscariot. As soon as Judas had received it Satan entered him. Jesus said to him, 'Do quickly what you have to do.' No one at the table understood what he meant by this. Some supposed that, as Judas was in charge of the common purse, Jesus was telling him to buy what was needed for the festival, or to make some gift to the poor. As soon as Judas had received the bread he went out. It was night (Jn. 13: 1-30). In all these notes on Judas, two things were clear; first, that he was the bursar, therefore, he was found to be trustworthy; second, he was especially concerned about the poor. Otherwise, he was not specified among the dull-headed, power-mongering and quarrelsome band of twelve disciples.

John writes later that according to Jesus Judas 'was doomed to be lost, for scripture has to be fulfilled' (17: 12). Although, this later verse, without taking seriously its scriptural indication of a personal friend turning against at a time of crisis, was taken to reaffirm the traditional view that Judas served an instrument of carrying out a divine plan in a universal drama, we have some revealing insights if we watch carefully some words and acts in the above description.

Jesus' washing of the disciples' feet and the subsequent conversation with them reveal his resisting to the temptation of power and authority and set an example of serving like slave as the mark of true divine authority. Here Judas is not projected as a bad guy after all, but someone who was confused about the demonstration of power in order to establish the reign of God. According to John, Judas' betrayal of Jesus did not involve the payment of thirty silver coins and kissing.

Judas' special relationship with Jesus and his popularity as someone committed to the cause of uplifting the poor made other disciples jealous of him. If his ultimate aim was to enjoy with thirty silver coins he could very well live on and enjoy life with that amount. Therefore it is most convincing to think that he wanted Jesus to overcome the enemies with using the miraculous powers and he betrayed him to see the drama happen at the time of arrest. And once it did not happen, the money appeared nothing, and hanged himself'. Again, the way he died is narrated in two different ways. According to Matthew, 'Judas threw the money into the temple and left. Then he went away and hanged himself' (Mt. 27: 5). But according to Luke, 'With the payment he received for his wickedness, Judas bought a field; there he fell headlong, his body burst open and all his intestines spilled out' (Acts 1: 18)!

1.17. There has been a tendency to single out a verse out of the context and build on a doctrine that can cause endless debates and weaken the evangelistic vigour. The belief in predestination may be a good example. Paul writes in the context of expounding 'present suffering and future glory': 'And we know that in all things God works for the good of those who love him, who have been called according to his purpose. For those God foreknew he also predestined to be conformed to the image of his Son, that he might be the firstborn among many brothers and sisters. And those he predestined, he also called; those he called, he also justified; those he justified, he also glorified' (Rom. 8: 29-30). Similarly, in the opening greeting in the epistle to Ephesians, we read: '(God) chose us in (Christ) before the creation of the world to be holy and blameless in his sight. In love predestined us for adoption to sonship through Jesus Christ, in accordance with his pleasure and will – to the praise of his glorious grace, which he has freely given to us in the One he loves' (1: 4-6). Seen from the religious language these passages reflect the specialist celebration of the new life, and God's love and hope with poetic touch. But in the Christian history, predestination became a matter of doctrinal position and it went to the extent of double predestination, that, God predestines some for eternal salvation and others for eternal damnation. Today, God's open grace and human will are affirmed together and thereby the biblical themes of repentance, new life, sharing the gospel and continued transformation become meaningful.

On the whole, the above problems found in the Bible, and many more if we go elaborately, need not undermine the sacred nature of God's Word written in human words with all human limitations. We do not believe in God dictating to one or individuals or giving visions to sages. God is extremely generous, gracious and humble in involving humans in revealing his word. The God-human collaboration in the making of the Bible gives enormous scope to deepen our spirituality, broaden our horizons and initiate creative actions. Above all, if carefully handled, the Christian scripture inspires and motivates the Christians and churches to move on in transformation.

2. Spirituality

2.1. There is a problem of the word 'spirituality' as it presupposes spirit separated from the matter. However, the advantage is not only its popular use (different terms in the vernacular) but also it suggests the pervasive nature of the Spirit throughout our life. It is based on divine presence as experienced by Adam and Eve in the garden Eden and Israelites during exodus and settlement. A psalmist succinctly puts it in a meaningful prayer: 'Where can I go from your Spirit? Where can I flee from your presence?' (Ps. 139: 7). As it is obvious that humans are spiritual beings, they have a transcendent urge; not satisfied with the material things. Then spirituality or living with mindfulness of God's presence always and everywhere does not dichotomize life as spiritual and material.

2.2. It is important to realize that Christians like some other religious communities do not believe in a soul which is completely separated from the body although the word 'soul' is used in the Bible which came from the Greek thought and translation. In the creation story we read that when formed the first man, God 'breathed into his nostrils the breath of life, and the man became a living being' (Gen. 2: 7). Therefore, the correct translation of the concerned Hebrew word is 'life force.' This life force permeates throughout our body and this is a basis for our belief in resurrection.

2.3. Jesus in his long prayer, recorded in John 17, asks the Father that not only his disciples may become one but also their unity is just like the unity between the Father and the Son, and they become one with Jesus-Father (Jn. 17: 20ff). This is most profound and challenging. This idea is extended to understand a Trinitarian spirituality. Although, the vision of God as one in three and three in one developed at the end of the biblical times its foundations are already there. We read of the Word, Spirit and God (Father) from the first book of the Bible. Their personal images, relational intimacy and working collaboration are tremendous. The Father and Son love each other while the source of love is the Spirit. The Spirit fills Jesus at his baptism when the heavenly Father attested. Both God the Father and the Son can send the Spirit which guides the Church. In the mission of liberation Jesus did what his Father was doing with the power of the Spirit. Jesus' disciples are called to join this dynamic unity, enjoy intimacy and work vigorously.

2.4. Unlike strict adherence to a tradition (e.g. in the case of Nicodemus) Christian life involves a born again experience: born of water, i.e. of mother's womb, and of spirit (or above); and be led by the Spirit which blows where she wills (Jn. 3). It is not a static life but moving one, being born again and again as new-born babes, in order to grow up in salvation (1 Pet. 2: 1-3).

2.5. Faith is fundamental to Christian spirituality. It should not be confused with a superficial piety and adherence to a set of beliefs or creed or tradition. Faith does have the connotations of trust, conviction and hope (Heb. 11: 1). More significant is the fact that according to Jesus it means the extraordinary ability to transcend, move on, to be able to break new ground, to dare the impossible etc. He appreciated certain people within his tradition as well as outside for having this faith (e.g. Mt. 8: 10; 9: 2; 9:22, 29; 1: 28; 16: 8; 19:20; Mk. 2: 5; Lk. 5: 20).

2.6. God is the source and inspiration for our faith. As he did in the case of the Hebrew slaves it is God who takes the initiative to liberate and accept. Jesus said, 'you did not choose me but I chose you.' As Paul expounds, we are saved by justification on the part of God in Christ and our response is a humble acceptance of it. Trying to persuade or move God is treachery and unfaithfulness. We are expected to live with the grateful attitude of being justified by faith and move on attempting great things for God's glory.

2.7. Faith without action is futile and the action is based on justice and caring the poor (James 2: 14-24). Jesus said that only by fruits one can distinguish between false prophets or disciples and the true ones. 'Every good tree bears good fruit, but a bad tree bears bad fruit' (Mt. 7: 17). John the Baptist rebukes those religious people who regarded baptism as an escape route to heaven. He asked for fruits of repentance and they included common people sharing their food and garments with those who did not have them, police (soldiers) not to extort or accuse anyone and be content with their salary and the tax collectors not to collect more than what was prescribed (Lk. 3: 7-14). Paul gives a list of the fruits of the Spirit: 'love, joy, peace, forbearance, kindness, goodness, faithfulness, gentleness and self-control (Gal. 5: 22f). These should be natural and spontaneous and any artificial efforts will expose hypocrisy.

2.8. Worshipping everywhere in spirit and truth is God's liking, according to Jesus (Jn. 4: 24); confining to particular place or building is parochial. Also there is a spiritual significance of coming together as a reconciled fellowship. Jesus said, 'Truly I tell you that if two of you on earth agree about anything they ask for, it will be done for them by my Father in heaven. For where two or three gather in my name, there am I with them' (Mt. 18: 19-20). Similarly, any offering to God without being reconciled with brothers and sisters will not be accepted (5: 23-24).

2.9. Prayer is the life line of Christian life. But asking for the physical and worldly needs is not primary in Christian prayer. Such prayer is common to all religious communities who believe in God or gods. When the disciples were concerned about their physical needs Jesus pointed out how God feeds the birds and clothes the flowers and added, 'And do not set your heart on what you will eat or drink; do not worry about it. For the pagan world runs after all such things, and the Father knows that you need them. But seek his kingdom, and these things will be given to you as well' (Lk. 12: 29-31; cf. Mt. 6: 8).

i. In his farewell speech of a poignant moment Jesus told his disciples, rather repeatedly, 'And I will do whatever you ask in my name, so that the Father may be glorified in the Son. You may ask me for anything in my name, and I will do it' (Jn. 14: 13f). Further this is connected with bearing fruit, the Father's love and loving each other (15: 16; 16: 23, 26). There is no clue for taking such verses as to present a catalogue of our daily needs to God. Here the meaning is assurance of support in exercising the discipleship in a hostile environment.

ii. Jesus taught that his disciples' prayer should not be like that of the public display of the hypocrites, nor should they keep on babbling like pagans; 'for they think they will be heard because of their many words.' Prayer should be done secretly (Mt. 6: 5-8).

iii. Christian prayer is of a unique character, that is, intimacy in relationship, talking clearly, seeking the will of God and growing in maturity and love. It is often quoted what Jesus said, 'Ask and it will be given to you; seek and you will find; knock and door will be opened to you' (Mt. 7: 7). This needs to be taken as general introduction to prayer and no one has experienced the literal meaning of it. Following the above introductory statement, Jesus said, 'Which of you, if your son asks for bread, will give him a stone? Or if he asks for a fish, give him a snake? If you, then, though you are evil, know how to give good gifts to your children, how much more will your Father in heaven give good gifts to those who ask him! (7: 9-10). Luke replaces 'good gifts' with 'the Holy Spirit' (11: 13)!

iv. In the context of chaos in Corinthian church, after explaining the limited value of gifts such as tongues, Paul writes: 'I will pray with my spirit, but I will also pray with my understanding; I will sing with my spirit, but I will also sing with my understanding...But everything should be done in a fitting and orderly way' (1 Cor. 14: 15, 40).

v. Persisting in prayer is often misplaced. A distorted understanding of Jesus' parable about a poor widow and unjust judge is taken as a guide for persisting, either personally or through mediation of a popular preacher, with shouting and fasting if it helps, with a view to move the unmoved, rock-like God. In actual fact, the plea of the widow is for justice, and the botheration and the possibility of final attack move the judge. Then Jesus comments that if in the case of an unjust judge such a change is possible, how much more quickly God will grant justice. Then he adds a footnote on the need of faith (ability to move) which was lacking in many people of his day (Lk. 18: 1-8).

2.10. The Lord's Prayer is a succinct model and template of authentic Christian prayer (Mt. 6: 9-13; Lk. 11; 2-4). There is an intimate affirmation of the heavenly Father (Mother and Companion). In a world where God's name is profaned by bloodshed and injustice, it should be hallowed by the faithful disciples. Seeking of God's reign and its coming is the primary purpose of prayer. So, also God's will may be done on earth as in the transcendent plane of heaven; and prayer does not change the will of God but it changes us to be in conformity to his will. Our daily bread is our daily need but not huge quantity for storing in greed. We constantly need God's forgiveness and there is a challenging condition that we forgive others who are indebted to us. In a world of fascinating and compelling temptations we need God's guidance and deliverance from the evil chains, both self-imposed and that from outside. As long as the supreme reign, power and glory are ascribed to God it is proper as they are not used for exploitation and domination.

2.11. We have already noted that asking for physical and worldly needs in many persuading ways including uttering mantras or names of God is common to all believers including Gentiles and pagans. There are some instances of stating the purpose of the prayer in a profound way. Let us consult Paul, the chief apostle, effective preacher and great pastor. For the Ephesian church he prays for the Spirit of wisdom and revelation to know God better, enlightenment for knowing the hope, the riches of the glorious inheritance, the power of resurrection and inner being, being rooted and established in love, power to grasp together with all the Lord's holy people, to grasp how wide and long and high and deep is the love of Christ and being filled to the measure of all the fullness of God (Ephe. 1: 15-21; 3: 14-19). To the Philippians he writes: 'This is my prayer: that your love may abound more and more in knowledge and depth of insight, so that you may be able to discern what is best and may be pure and blameless for the day of Christ, filled with the fruit of righteousness that comes through Jesus Christ – to the glory and praise of God' (Phil. 1: 9-11). In the case of Colossians the prayer is for being filled with God's will 'through all the wisdom and understanding that the Spirit gives, so that you may live life worthy of the Lord and please him in every way: bearing fruit in every good work, growing in the knowledge of God, being strengthened with all power according to his glorious might so that you may have great endurance and patience' (Col. 1: 1-11). It will be a rewarding exercise to compare the stated purposes of prayer here with those offered by pastors and preachers.

2.12. We should be careful not to violate the commandment of not misusing God's name (Ex. 20: 7). When we pray in Jesus' name we affirm our affinity to him and our conformity to his character and will. This is true of performing miracles also. For example, Jesus said, 'Not everyone who says to me, "Lord, Lord," will enter the kingdom of heaven, but only the one who does the will of my Father who is in heaven. Many will say to me on that day, "Lord, Lord, did we not prophesy in your name and in your name drive out demons and in your name perform many miracles?" Then I will tell them plainly, "I never knew you. Away from me, you evil doers!"' (Mt. 7: 21-23). Following a miracle of restoring wholeness to a crippled by the name of Jesus, in answer to a pressing query, Peter said that Jesus' was the only name for salvation (sound health or wholeness – Acts 4; 1-12). There is a dramatic yet telling story in Acts 19: 13-16 of seven exorcists who used the name of Jesus with a wrong motive and the evil spirits overpowered them and they ran away naked!

2.13. Speaking in tongs was a controversial phenomenon in the early church. It happened in the unexpected and instant pouring of the Spirit on the Pentecostal day (Acts 2). It was a miracle in which those who heard could hear in their own tongues. In any case the event was followed by the formation of a church where resources were equally shared. Later, speaking in tongues as a gift of the Spirit became a problem in the Corinthian church. Paul deals with this issue in 1 Cori. 12-14. First, he acknowledges different kinds of gifts but he insists that they are given for common good. He gives a list of nine gifts and the last three are distinguishing between spirits, speaking in different kind of tongues and interpretation of tongues. Then he argues for different functions within the same body, the church. Then he asks, 'do all speak tongues and do all interpret?' The greatest gift, he says, is love which is indispensable. Further, he takes up the question of intelligibility in worship where speaking an unknown tongue is just speaking into the air. There is no language in the world without meaning. Therefore one who speaks in tongues should pray for ability to interpret. Praying and singing should be governed by spirit and understanding. After, stressing that five intelligible words in the church are more useful than many tongues, Paul exhorts: 'Brothers and sisters, stop thinking like children. In regard to evil be infants, but in your thinking be adults' (14: 20). By quoting a verse from the Hebrew scripture, he says that 'Tongues, then, are a sign, not for believers but for unbelievers.' Also he reasons that when enquirers or unbelievers come to a church where everyone speaks in tongues they will say 'you are out of your mind.' Paul's final allowance is that up to three persons can speak tongues in a worship, one at a time, and someone must interpret – all within order and decency.

2.14. Miracles do happen but miracle by definition is something unexpected and unpredictable. Jesus and the apostles never gave publicity and miraculous events just happened instantly and incidentally. They always interpreted them as the sign of the inbreaking of God's reign in the world in which, as expected, 'the blind receive sight, the lame walk, those who have leprosy are cleansed, the deaf hear, the dead are raised, and the good news is proclaimed to the poor' (Mt. 11: 5; cf. Is. 35: 5-6; 61: 1-2; Lk. 4: 18-19). In some cases Jesus told the healed not to tell anyone lest they would misunderstand. We have some extraordinary preachers who have the gift of healing but keep it secret and if necessary even give up. Any campaigns of miracles with commercial purpose with manipulative adverts, over-projecting few cases of success with well-prepared testimonies and ignoring the majority cases of failure who are pushed to further frustration, become a scandal.

2.15. In spiritual life we have an equanimity of mind. We don't over rejoice on success not become despondent of failure. God's providence and guidance is not always deterministic. However, at any crisis, God provides new possibilities for us to work with sincerely. One of the best examples is the story of Naomi and Ruth; two frustrated widows with bitterness work together for a new chapter in their life and finally both find a shared blessing, a new life which had perennial significance.

2.16. Christian spirituality finds most authentic expression when we respond to God's call in love and commit ourselves to discipleship and mission. It is a life of simplicity and self-denial. It is not a jolly life craving to grab fashions, fancies, glamour and consumer excess. Of course, there will be food on the way and friends to enjoy fellowship. But our focus will be on the Trinitarian God who in a dynamic unity continues to act creatively and longs to have fellowship with humanity.

2.17. Spirituality is ongoing transformation in Christian life. It is a life born-again and again (Jn. 3: 3, 5; 1 Pet. 2: 1-3) experiencing transforming glory after glory (2 Cori. 3: 17). It is arrogant to claim that we know Christ on the basis of a cerebral knowing of some recorded facts in Sunday School or theological college. Paul considers everything a loss because of the surpassing greatness of knowing Christ, knowing the power of resurrection and participation in his sufferings, and pressing on 'to take hold of that for which Christ Jesus took hold of me' (Phil. 3: 8ff). This is a stunning realization which could be shared by every Christian. The unlimited and unending possibilities in a Christian journey makes spirituality exciting and motivates for participating in God's ongoing mission in Christ's way.

3. Faith Formulations and Expressions

3.1. Unlike any other religious traditions, Christianity has two main creeds, Apostles' Creed and Nicene Creed. We use them in worship services though there is a difference from denomination to denomination about the frequency. As we know from history, the creeds were produced after long debates in church councils in the early centuries of the history of church.

3.2. Are the creeds sufficient to communicate the Christian faith? A detailed analysis can be made in Christian group discussions. For example, why there is no mention of the decisive experience of the Hebrews/Israelites/Jews which is narrated in about three fourth of the Bible? And why there is no mention of the life and ministry of Jesus as a Jew? One convincing answer is that the early Church Fathers and political rulers who were responsible for the creation and authorization of the creeds were anti-Jewish and we have external evidence too for this fact. The Reformation did not rectify this flaw as Martin Luther and some of his colleagues were also anti-Jewish. The Christian–Jewish enmity has had tragic events and serious repercussions even today.

3.3. Though it may be rejected by Indian Christians on the whole, some have come to the conclusion that for the sake of the comprehensiveness of the Christian faith, new statements of faith can be created. Thus, there are new faith affirmations created and used in worship services, mainly in theological institutions.

3.4. As we read in the New Testament, Jesus was a multifaceted figure. He was a devout Jew, teacher and prophet, was confessed as Son of God, Son of Man, Christ (Messiah) and interpreted as the enfleshment of the eternal, cosmic, divine Word. He claimed to be one with the heavenly Father in terms of intimate relationship and conformity with the Father's will and purpose. Further, he was conceived as the revelation of the Son aspect (person) of the Triune God along with the Father and the Holy Spirit. But today this clarity is not evident in our worship and preaching. There is a Jesus cult dominant and outsiders also say that we worship Jesus as our personal and favoured deity. This confusion has to be removed for the clarity of the Christian faith. Some groups emphasize the work of the Holy Spirit without touching the Father and Son.

3.5. The Holy Spirit is another aspect (person) of the Trinity. The Holy Spirit throughout the Bible is witnessed as the creative, living and moving Spirit. The Spirit who filled the leaders and prophets, also filled Jesus who in turn breathed the Spirit on the disciples. The manifestation of the Spirit on the Pentecost was a great miracle to continue the Christian movement. The Spirit gave the disciples and believers wisdom and power, gifts and guidance. There may be times of ecstasy and excitement but any emotional manipulation and unreasonable behavior would distort the image and function of the Spirit.

3.6. The image Father is taken as the image of the Godhead. At times the Father represents the hierarch in the Trinitarian unity but an exemplary hierarch with love and openness to recognize the work of others and glorify them. Jesus expressed the hierarchical highness and relational oneness in terms of 'my Father is greater than me and 'I and the Father are one.' The Spirit is seen as the one who goes between them and joins them in a dynamic movement.

3.7. Trinity cannot be understood by arithmetic calculations though we say one in three and three in one. One possibility is to present the unique vision of Trinity as creative and dynamic. Imagine the rotation of three figures mounted on a display board. In the fast moving we see only one figure but in slow motion we see three. A tri-colored diamond in rotation also gives similar perception. We need to celebrate both the individual work of each and joint work of all the three. Taking out one and project as the only one may be construed as idol worship. Trinity is a divine commune or community of divinities whose mysterious presence can be experienced in moving corporately as in a group dance or as working together with genuine commitment and love in a church.

3.8. Christian faith is informed and shaped by the stories and experiences of God's people throughout the Bible. For example, Abraham was called to be a blessing in terms of setting new values in a corrupt society. He gave priority to his junior nephew, refused to accept the booty from the king Sodom following a battle and refused to receive a cave free to bury his wife. As a liberated and covenanted community, the Hebrews were called to establish a model community based on justice, peace and love. When they forgot and drifted away the prophets reprimanded them, presented God in solidarity with the victims and presented a picture of hope for the coming of the Messiah who would fulfill the original purpose of God's calling of his people. In the context of many claiming to be the Messiah, Jesus fulfilled the prophesy by giving solidarity with the victims of injustice and they included the disabled, lepers, women with bad name, the poor and those alienated such as the tax collectors for various reasons.

3.9. As we noted earlier Jesus gave a new definition of faith, which fundamentally means the ability to transcend, to move on, (e.g. moving mountain, uprooting tree, mustard seed to sprout etc.). What does it mean for those of us who claim to have faith in him? There can be a measure of faith, which could be great or little (Rom. 12: 3; Mt. 8: 26; 15: 28; 17:20). It should be our prayer, 'Lord, increase our faith' (Lk. 17: 5). To those who failed to persist on the pursue of justice Jesus said, 'when the Son of Man comes, will he find faith on earth?' (18: 8). Without our faith God cannot do anything. Therefore, in whatever way we formulate our faith and express it in a particular context, faith in its dynamic sense should inform us.

3.10. Fundamental to all the above is, to be open to the unfolding of the reality as we feel in our life, while reading the Bible and reading non-biblical texts. Paul states this succinctly as ongoing transformation (2 Cor. 3: 18), having the power to know the height, length, width and depth of the love of God (Eph. 3: 17-19) and growing in the knowledge of Christ (Phil. 3: 7-11). In this process there is no room to boast about any status in faith and level of understanding. In this sense, no openness means no salvation.

4. The Defining Characteristics of Evangelical Faith

4.1. Evangelism means preaching the good news. Jesus preached the good news to the poor that the incoming reign of God belonged to them. And also as we have already stated , he preached the good news of acceptance to all those who were alienated in the society for various reasons. The apostles extended the purview of the good news to cover all sorts of people, both those with self-imposed chains and those who suffered bondage to sin. Paul crystalized the good news with a focus on God's gracious acceptance of all persons irrespective of their moral, physical, mental and social conditions and a call to repent and accept this acceptance and living a new life. Fundamentalism in any form is opposed to evangelism although many fundamentalists play a strategy and call themselves evangelicals.

4.2. As we stated above, Christian faith is not static with strict following of some norms, traditions and rules. It is open to new perceptions and possibilities. From their life, thought and ministry some inspiring preachers, ministers and leaders, we learn that the more one is evangelical the more s/he is radical, and the more one is radical the more s/he is ecumenical. In Ezekiel 37, first we read about the picture of the revival of dry bones signifying a new life for people; second, the coming together of Israel and Judah (two sticks bound together). Jesus in his last prayer for his disciples just before his death said 'that all of them may be one as we are one so that the world may believe that you have sent me' (Jn. 17: 21). This verse has inspired many to work for church unity and union including the Church of South India (1947), the first united church of its kind in the history of Christianity.

4.3. Basically our life should reflect the evangelical (good news) faith and our neighbours of other faiths or no faith discreetly watch and observe us, and assess fruits of the new life we claim. 'Look at Christians, how they love one another' is a traditional testimony by outsiders. If we attack, create noise and bear false witness against our neibhours we poison our evangelical witness.

4.4. There is so much of religiosity and piety in India among all religious communities. Approaching God for immediate benefits and eternal rest is also common. Can Christians claim that their Jesus-deity is of greater power to bestow blessings and shot cut way to heaven? We can inspire others only through our action for change in good and genuine spirit. When we make our colleagues, neighbours and friends find in us the Jesus-like life miraculous change may happen. Then there will be greater credibility for what we do and say.

4.5. Our words must be governed by the principle of 'yes' or 'no' as taught by our Lord. We need to be accurate, honest without twist and undue exaggeration. It is popularly observed that purity of heart, mind and hand is the basic criterion for a decent life. Artificial smile and a pious slang of speech is not a substitute!

4.6. We need to have symbols and structures that reflect on the love of God and love for fellow humans. Leadership and management is the primary area for evangelization. Particularly, if the church elections are not held in a decent and prayerful manner what we preach will be discredited. Also, one important area where we are expected to be evangelical is the way we administer. It should reflect the evangelical values of honesty, fairness, transparency, justice, courtesy and love.

5. Challenges of Conservatism and Fundamentalism

5.1. The greatest challenges for evangelical faith is conservatism and fundamentalism. Conservatism safeguards the tradition in the past established mainly by the western missionaries. Church buildings which they wrongly called temples in the vernacular continue to be built in the same design. Liturgies, hymns and the patterns of ministry continue from this tradition. Even a proof reading of what they produced are not allowed. We have a set of hymns on the occasions of wedding, funeral etc and there is no encouragement for producing new meaningful songs but fundamentalist songs with simple and lively music but superficial ideas are accommodated. It should be our firm position that the God who worked in the history of Israel, western Christianity and missionaries is with us, among us and in our local area, calling us to be faithful and credible witnesses.

5.2. Conservatism is not only the trait of Christianity. In other religions as well there are elements of it. For example, we see certain rituals and ceremonies which have been repeated by Hindu priests for centuries. The concerned community believes that what was revealed to sages thousands of years ago is sacred and eternal truth and therefore the more accurately they are performed the more effective they are. Some others may worship and pray in the same patterns as it was instructed by the founder of their religion. In what way Christian conservatism is different?

5.3. Today it is often said that change is the only constant. Though with little grudge at the beginning, we have accepted new electronic devices, medical facilities, scientific developments, renaissance of language, new fashions of dress and hair style, new types of food etc. But if we do not come forward to revise our liturgies and popular Bible translations we unconsciously hinder the communication of the gospel with the present generation.

5.4. Liturgical renewal can promote renewal of Christian life and the life of the church. Good liturgies convey the distinctive character of the gospel. If we are open we find meaningful liturgies produced across the world and they are ecumenical too. In India we have uniquely rich resources to use for new liturgies and contribute to the world wide church.

5.5. There are Christians who still believe that the original revelation of the word of God was through their mother tongue. They do not know the history and number of translations in their language. Where there is linguistic renaissance in their state they have no other way than accepting it and training themselves in speaking and writing in the new vocabulary and style. Particularly, the young generation of students study in good language but they are either forced or encouraged to read the old translation of the Bible and speak in its style. Because of this stubborn fact they are not able to communicate the Christian message to their friends and peer groups.

5.6. We may say that we have got used to a liturgical pattern and particular translation of the Bible and because of the familiarity we have internalized the meaning and, to change is very difficult. If so, we have to ask the question how much change a person from other faith will undergo if s/he decides to become a Christian. Only in the context of our ongoing change, we can expect change from others.

5.7. There is no need to change for the sake of change. But our own self-understanding and understanding of others change is indispensable. We have several stories of Christians betraying their debilitating ignorance before others. Knowing the truth gives an experience of liberation and clear communication. Those who have engaged in Bible studies and some form of theological education with the help of the theologically trained persons come with excitement about what they have learned. If we do not have the urge and openness to know how can we dare to teach the truth in our mission fields? Let us remember Jesus' challenge to the conservative Jews, his slow-thinking disciples for knowing and understanding the new truth.

5.8. We have already noted calling wrongly the church building as temple. It is the unique idea that God's dwelling place is among the people. Building a temple became controversial in Israel though the temple in Jerusalem occupied the central place of the Jewish community including those in the Diaspora. Just like prophets like Jeremiah were, Jesus was critical of the temple building and was accused for foretelling its destruction. In any case, just like the original temple of Solomon was destroyed by the Babylonian army in the late sixth century BCE the later temple was destroyed by the Roman army in the early 70s of the first century CE. Early Christians worshiped in homes, catacombs, beaches and river banks. When the Church came under the Roman Empire huge basilicas and churches were built. In the context of the alliance between the State and the Church, parallel to the palaces, cathedrals were built as the seats (*cathedra*) of bishops. But Reformation helped to go back to the simple apostolic understanding but it could not resist the human pride in having big buildings and identifying them with Solomon's temple. With this mistaken identity church leaders appeal persuasively and people give generously while for social engagement their contribution is minimal if not nil. In a country with spectacular temples, mosques and gurudwaras, our simple church buildings will communicate the distinctive Christian message of God's special presence in the midst of a gathered congregation.

5.9. In relation to the above, in the traditions of temple-like churches the leaders are called priests. Jesus was never called a priest and the writer to the Hebrews interprets him as a peculiar figure as both the high priest and the victim in a spiritual sacrifice. And there is no office or title of a priest in the order of ministry in the New Testament. In the Reformed Churches words like presbyter, pastor and minister are used. In the recent discussions the idea of servant (minister) with necessary modifications according to the roles is emphasized. Suitable uniforms also should be decided accordingly. The biblical idea of 'collective priesthood' or 'priesthood of all believers' (Ex. 19: 6; 1 Pet. 2: 9) has yet to find its fullest expression.

5.10. If ministry in an area is collective the 'minister' does not play the central role but coordinating role. Lay members should have more participation in the ministry of the Word, sacrament, home visits and social engagement, not simply offering a prayer, reading the scripture lessons and collecting and counting the offertory. Only ministers with clarity, courage and confidence can ensure this happen. Further, not only worship services including ceremonies on different occasion – baptism, Eucharist, wedding, funeral etc - and home visits, but also social engagement depending on the local situation is indispensable in Christian witness. Individuals fighting injustice may become vulnerable to revengeful reaction but church's solidarity will be a great force.

6. The Church of Confession, Service and Witness

6.1. The Christian church is in continuation of the Hebrew community which was formed following their liberation from the slavery in Egypt. God made a covenant with them which was conditioned by faithfulness and obedience to the commandments. It was a great socio-religious experiment with a view to provide a model for all communities which was to be fascinating. The community of God's people was based on justice, peace, love and sharing of resources.

6.2. The people of God were numerically small and weak (Deut. 7: 7). Jesus' disciples were a little flock (Lk. 12: 32) and asked to be light and salt, minority symbols. Paul tells the Corinthians that many of them were not wise by human standards, influential and of noble birth (1 Cori. 1: 26). 'But God chose the foolish things of the world to shame the wise; God chose the weak things of the world to shame the strong' (1: 27). Therefore, we are not supposed to pride on numerical strength and other influential positions. In most cases church being majority has proved to be dangerous with conflicts and wars. Christian minority in India is often reminded not to be nervous and agitative but creative and contributing. Even when ridiculed and harassed by religio-political majority, we have encouraging words, 'fear not, little flock; I am with you always.' Persecution may happen but we should not invite it by our unwise behaviour (1 Pet. 2: 19-20).

We need to have the combination of the intelligence of the serpents and innocence of the doves (Mt. 10: 16).

6.3. The Hebrew community of God's people had to struggle to take decisions on issues such as kingship, temple, sacrifices and priesthood. Instead of attracting the neighbouring communities they were attracted by the latter and this led to a great fall. Original vision and ideals could not be realized. For example, because of kings the norm of re-sharing resources at every fiftieth year could not see its day. Instead of welcoming strangers and liberating domestic slaves at the seventh year with provisions for a wholesome life, they were exploited. Violence, bloodshed, adultery, having unlimited number of wives and heavy taxation particularly in the rule of the kings David and Solomon took the nation to a shameful downfall.

6.4. In the face of a socio-economic depression and religio-moral degradation prophets arose as the spokespersons of God. They pointed out the community's faithlessness and unjust practices from market places to royal courts and called people for repentance and new orientation in life. They supported the few kings (e.g. Josiah) who initiated reformation and dealt the poor with justice. Covenant renewals happened and there was vision for an eternal covenant which guaranteed law written in hearts making preachers redundant (Jer. 31: 31ff). They also presented a vision of hope for the establishment of a Messianic community which would fulfill the ideals of the original expectation of the community.

6.5. Jesus called a group of twelve disciples and connected their role with the twelve tribes of Israel. They were socially insignificant and economically poor. Jesus wanted to demonstrate that only the weak and poor can represent the cause of those who were lost, least and last. Jesus' death appeared to shatter the hope for establishing a new community. But his resurrection from the dead gave a new experience of hope for the disciples, men and women, and sustained their hope by being together and sharing fellowship.

6.6. Following the unexpected outpouring of the Holy Spirit on one festival Pentecost celebrated, Peter preached a fiery sermon on repentance, forgiveness and baptism. 'About three thousand were added to their number on that day' (Acts 2: 4). What followed were suggesting a decisive moment in the formation and growth of the church. They devoted to apostles' teaching, sharing fellowship with breaking bread, holding every possession including property in common, praising God and enjoying the favour of the people. More people were added to their fellowship (2: 42-47). The number of 'disciples' were increasing and there was already the problem of catering to the need of all fairly (6: 1). 'The disciples were called Christians first at Antioch' (11: 26). The name change did warrant the identity and character of disciples.

6.7. It is not clear whether Jesus intended to establish a church as we know it today. However, there are glimpses into his desire for creating a sacred fellowship following the original vision of his Jewish tradition for a covenanted community or the people of God with collective priesthood and being light for other nations by following the wise law they received (Ex. 19: 6; Deut. 4: 6-8). Jesus called a group of disciples, taught them the values of God's reign and tried to sanctity them. There are references to the fact that the sanctity of the church lies in the unity of its members. E.g. Before offering the gifts to the altar one should get reconciled with brothers and sisters (Mt. 5: 23-24). Sins and cases can be dealt within the church (18: 15-18). If there is agreement between members the Father will give what they ask for (18: 19). 'For where two or three gather in my name, there am I with them (18: 20).

6.8. The early disciples or Christians met in houses and they were collectively called as the household of God built on the foundation of the apostles and prophets with Jesus as the corner stone. As people of God and fellow citizens we are a building and joined together and rise to become a holy temple in the Lord in which God lives by the Holy Spirit (Eph. 2: 19-22). Today the church building provides a space for gathering for worship and planning or coordinating mission. It may also be a space to welcome strangers.

6.9. The symbols building, temple, flock, collective priesthood, vine etc are applicable to the church provided Christians are clear about the purpose of their calling and commitment as children of God, disciples of Jesus and temples of the Spirit. As salt, light and good fruit bearing trees they are supposed to be a fascinating community. What matters most is not individual piety or collective piety controlled by a charismatic individual, but unity which defines its sanctity as we have noted above. A building's strength rests on its integrity (1 Pet. 2: 8-9). Body is a popular image in the New Testament. Here the integrity of the limbs defines the health and function of the body. Gifts are different and roles are different and when all of them are integrated into the body of the church it serves the purpose of its existence (Rom. 12: 3-8; 1 Cori. 12: 12-29).

6.10. Temptation of power and misuse of authority can poison the holy fellowship of the church. Jesus himself overcame that temptation and tried his best to make his disciples understand the counter-cultural values of God's reign. When two disciples wanted to have the right-left sides of Jesus in his glory, which created tension within the band, Jesus called them together and gave them the mula-matra: Unlike among the Gentiles, 'whoever wants to become great among you must be your servant, and whoever wants to be first must be slave of all. For even the Son of Man did not come to be served, but to serve, and to give his life as a ransom for many' (Mk. 10: 43-45). But until the end they were power mongering asking when will the kingdom will come so that they would sit on thrones to judge people of Israel or aspire the left side and right side of Jesus, the Christ. Towards the end of his life Jesus was once again tempted by the thought of having authority over the world and of going to the Father, the source of all power. He conquered it by instantly washing the feet of his disciples and asked them to do the same (Jn. 13: 1-17). It was a stunning demonstration of the profound truth that the beauty of authority lies in serving others as servants or slaves, not without dignity.

6:11. In Christian ministry the ministering and pastoral elements were shared corporately. 'Priests' are not mentioned as a category of Christian workers as all believers are priests (Rom. 12: 6-7; 1 Cor. 12: 27-30; Eph. 4: 11-13; 1 Pet. 2: 9). Interestingly, while apostles and prophets are on the top of the list given in the texts just quoted, leaders and administrators come towards the last! Pastors/presbyters/ministers are servants of the congregation as well as the local community and there is no central and ruling role but equipping and coordinating one. To offer for administrative or leadership role is a noble thing provided there is no aspiration or vested interest. According to the revolutionary teaching of Jesus, whoever takes the lowly position of a child (powerless yet powerful in love) is the greatest in the kingdom of heaven (Mt. 18: 4). No amount of piety and no length of prayer can be a substitute for a child-like life and leadership.

6.12. The church is expected to set an inspiring model of servant-hood. Outsiders need to know that we are vested by God through Jesus not with a crusading mind but a crucified mind. Filled with the Spirit and fear of God, justice and peace, transparency and accountability, the genuine leaders witness to the fundamentals of the gospel. Dust-emitting and party-based election campaigns with conflicts of interests damage the Christian witness. The experiment of the early apostles suggests an alternative (Acts 1). Today some Christian leaders of international repute fascinate the world community through their simplicity, humility, service and concern for peace among communities and nations, and protection of the environment.

6.13. Teaching the Christians is an important aspect of ministry. In India we witness swelling crowds of pilgrims even with a risk of being killed in stampede or flood. While showing serious solidarity with the victims, Christians should be able to distinguish between piety and faith, to celebrate the divine grace by which they are saved, and to enjoy the direct access to approach and address God as Father (and Mother). Most distinctively, they are called to a new life and a commitment to participate in God's continuing mission. They need to be careful of the false prophets and pompous preachers about whom Jesus warned his disciples.

6.14. The church's ministry should not be limited to worship services, home visits etc. They should engage in issues facing the local community. For example, to address the ambiguous behaviour of the youth there might be a programme of recreation and counseling; a day care centre might be operated for the elderly; good understanding might be maintained with the local police, revenue authorities etc. By participating in campaigns on issues of justice and interfaith harmony the Christian community must show that God cares for all and is in solidarity with the victims and the vulnerable.

7. Mission and Evangelism

7.1. It is the fundamental duty of every Christian to participate in God's mission wherever they live or are sent. This mission is in connection with a long chain with different focal points. The ancestors of Israel, particularly Abraham, were called to be a blessing in their nomadic context. As their stories suggest, they were against any form of exploitation by money power, muscle power and moral power. They had extraordinary faith to move in an adventurous journey. Moses was called to go on a mission of liberating the Hebrew slaves from Egypt, leading them in the wilderness and settling them down in Canaan. He also was an instrument of God's covenant with the Hebrew community which involved in being faithful to God and establishing a model community according to the laws and precepts.

7.2. The Hebrew prophets played a unique role by challenging unjust authorities and exploiting systems. They assured the nervous faithful people of God's presence with them, called the unfaithful for repentance and a new life, and reminded the community of their odyssey in the past. When kingship in Israel turned to be divisive and destructive (as was originally warned) they envisioned an anointed one (Messiah) who will have the Spirit of wisdom, understanding, counsel, power, knowledge and fear of the Lord (Is. 11: 2). They forecast an eternal covenant and a new heaven and new earth.

7.3. John the Baptist transited the mission of the Hebrew prophets (particularly, Elijah) to address a new situation. He was out of the customary norms, fashions and styles. His message in the wilderness was not abstract but concrete appealing to specific situation. He called 'brood of vipers' those who took religious rites like baptism an escape route from danger. He asked them not to boast of themselves as children of Abraham as God was able to create such children out of the 'stones', insignificant people. He asked for repentance and fruit bearing life. Again, he was specific about action: common people should share cloths and food with others; tax collectors should not collect more than required and the police men ('soldiers') should not extort money and accuse people falsely but be content with their pay (Lk. 3: 7-14). Those who are passionate to be in mission in India would find the catalogue of such people is much longer. Finally, for daring to challenge the immoral king Herod for keeping his wife, John was beheaded (Mk. 7: 17-29). His legacy in mission is powerful.

7.4. Jesus first shared his mission with John proclaiming 'The time has come. The kingdom of God is near. Repent and believe the good news' (Mk. 1: 15; cf. Mt. 3: 2). Just like John, Jesus also connected his mission with the mission and vision of the Hebrew prophets. His Nazareth manifesto (Lk. 4: 18ff) includes preaching good news to the poor, proclaiming freedom for the prisoners and recovery of sight for the blind, releasing the oppressed and proclaiming the year of the Lord's favour. He had a specific focus of mission, i.e., the lost sheep of Israel, all those who were marginalized among Jewish Diaspora, including the disabled, alienated, women, lepers and children. His miracles and parables pointed out the possibility of a new life. It so happened that he extended the boundary of his ministry when challenged by certain outsiders (Mt. 15: 21-28). He confronted the conservative wing of his community who refused 'to move on' which was the meaning of faith (Mk. 2: 5; 10: 52; Mt. 9: 22; Lk. 17: 5, 56).

7.5. Jesus trained his disciples for continuing his mission. His basic formula of commissioning was, 'As the Father has sent me, I am sending you' (Jn. 20: 21; 17: 18). There was no agenda or constitution of an organised programme. Basically they had to be open to the guidance of the Holy Spirit and continue the mission of their master: preaching the gospel, healing the sick and challenging the unjust powers. Further, the following four versions of the Great Commission, add specific elements in the character and purpose of mission.

7.6. According to Matthew (28: 16-20), the commission was given in an unknown mount in Galilee thus contrasting the expectation that the word of God would come from the mount of Zion or Jerusalem (Is. 2: 2; Mic. 2: 2). Making disciples, baptizing in the triune name of God and teaching everything Jesus had commanded, were the main activities. The promise was Jesus' constant presence with them. Mark notes 'going into all the world and preach the gospel to all creation.' Salvation of those who believed and extraordinary signs of their belief are added (16: 15ff). Luke write: '...repentance for the forgiveness of sins will be preached in his (Messiah) name to all nations, beginning at Jerusalem. You are witnesses of these things' (24: 7-48). For John, the commissioning was more dramatic: Showing the wounded hands and side to his disciples, Jesus breathed on them and said, 'Receive the Holy Spirit. If you forgive anyone's sins, their sins are forgiven; if you do not forgive them, they are not forgiven' (20: 20-23). The background of the last words was that Jesus as the Son of Man, in solidarity with and representing the victims of injustice, claimed authority to forgive sins (Mt. 9: 6). The disciples are vested with the same authority provided they followed their master. There is no external authority from above to forgive.

7.7. What is gospel? There is no evidence to take it as one word, idea or one time pill. If we take a survey of the changing meanings of and foci of the gospel in the NT we may come to the conclusion that we can reasonably talk in terms of gospel stories, gospel insights, gospel values, gospel works and so on. It is not difficult to notice in the Bible changing perceptions and articulations depending on the contexts. For example, in the context of return from the exile in Babylon in the sixth century BCE Isaiah says, 'How beautiful on the mountains are the feet of those who bring good news, who proclaim peace, bring good tidings, who proclaim salvation, who say to Zion, "your God reigns!"' (Is. 52: 7). The contents of the good news in this passage are repeated themes both in the Hebrew scripture and the New Testament (Rom. 10: 15). Connected with are God's compassion and love, and God's solidarity with the victims, as evident in the stories of Cain-Abel, liberation-exodus and prophets' cry.

7.8. Jesus and John the Baptist preached awareness of God's reign, repentance and belief in the gospel (Mt. 3: 2; Mk. 1: 15). Repentance is preached to corrupt officials, rulers and rich persons. In Luke Jesus' multiple task of communicating the good news is presented as the fulfilment of Isaiah: 'The Spirit of the Lord is on me, because he has anointed me to proclaim good news to the poor. He has sent me to proclaim the freedom for the prisoners and recovery of the sight for the blind, to set the oppressed free, to proclaim the year of the Lord's favour' (Lk. 4: 18-19; cf. Is. 61: 1-2; note 'the day of vengeance' in Isaiah is omitted in Luke!). The acts of liberation were interpreted as the best practices of religion, the true fasting (Is. 58: 6) and Jesus quoted them for the frustrated Baptist as evidence of the arrival of the Messianic age. We have already noted the elements of the gospel in the four versions of the Great Commission.

7.9. In the Acts of the Apostles, apart from the teachings of repentance, Holy Spirit, salvation (holistic), deliverance by healing, telling the Hebrew story (Stephen's sermon), good news about Jesus, the suffering servant etc. and that God raised him from the dead was the central message (2: 32; 13: 30; 17: 31). It should be rewarding to re-read the Acts and note down all the references to the gospel and meaning. One may be tempted to proclaim Jesus Christ as the gospel, but the Gospels and Acts present Jesus as rooted in Hebrew/Jewish tradition though his significance was perceived as new when related to the Greek and Roman traditions.

7.10. To the Jews the apostles confessed Jesus mainly as the Christ. But Christ was not expected by Romans and Greeks, therefore, the titles Saviour and Lord dominated in their preaching to them. There arose a problem, and the question was whether the Gentile Christians had to go through the Jewish customs such as circumcision. Some Jewish Christians insisted on observing this and other laws. Paul developed a new focus, i.e. justification by faith which he expounds in his letters to the Romans and Galatians. For him it was grounded on the Hebrew tradition, particularly in the life of Abraham. The gist of the meaning of the justification by faith is, 'God has accepted you by grace in love irrespective of your condition, and you accept this and lead a new life.' This focus caused two risky tendencies. First, the Gentile Christians tended to undermine the significance of the Jewish tradition and the noble ideal of the law. Immediately Paul tried to pull them from the other end and established the significance of the Jewish tradition for Christian faith as we read in Rom. 9-11. Second, there was a tendency to neglect fruitful life including justice and righteousness in the name of grace. Paul insists on good works as a natural consequence of the experience of justification by faith (Rom. 6, Gal. 5). More glaringly, James in his letter denounces faith without work and turns to the Hebrew prophets for wisdom and justice. This is a good example of keeping the appeal of the gospel in dialectic tension depending on the context.

7.11. In their context of struggle against the imperial cult of Rome and the Empire's oppressive policies and exploitative trade the Christians of the Asia Minor projected Jesus as the lion-turned lamb, with perfect authority and universal presence, but remaining slain, slain from the creation of the world (Rev. 5: 6; 13: 8). Moreover, the last book gives a definition of the 'eternal gospel' – 'fear God and give him glory' (14: 6-7). Throughout the Bible 'fearing God' is mentioned as a basic response to God which finds expression in loving God and doing justice.

7.12. Instead of uncritically glorifying western missionaries and their achievements and of boasting of the denominational identity therewith, Christians in India should proclaim God as present always and everywhere in India as elsewhere. They have been presented the recent ecumenical thrust of 'mission in Christ's way' and openness on the continuing journey focusing on new thrusts in particular contexts. Mission in Christ's way with openness in India requires the recapturing of the multi-dimensional and integrated character of mission. It is a transforming mission, covering cultures, caste divisions, political systems, population explosion, poverty, untouchability and communal conflicts. Gender equality, child rights and corruption free administration cannot go on untouched by the challenges of Christ's mission. The dangerous process of politicization of religion and communalization of politics needs to be countered by challenge and positive action. It is an evangelical act to participate in national integration and reconstruction, to join activities of pollution control and participation in the present 'Clean India' programme.

7:13. It is important to deconstruct the meaning of horrible expressions such as that Jesus as the sacrificial lamb was slaughtered in order to appease or satisfy the wrathful and blood thirsty God, and we are washed in the blood of Christ. Some missionaries have presented them as symbolic expressions of God's suffering in solidarity with sinners and victims of injustice. A study of different interpretations of the cross evident in the New Testament (e.g. reconciliation, climax of the incarnational humility and exposing the naked power and nailing it) would reveal different interpretations of the cross.

7.14. Local church is the locus of mission. Prophet Isaiah received a call to work in the local area though the text (ch. 6) is read in services of commissioning for mission overseas! Jesus asked his disciples to share the gospel on their way in day to day life although he hinted out its rippling out to larger region (Judea, Samaria) and unto the end of the world. A local church which fails to be a living outreach in its local community is not fit for sending missionaries to faraway places. It is a grave sin to talk about and send out for mission with a hidden view to conceal the political sewage of sending bodies. Vision for Equipping Local Churches for Mission (VELCOM) was a novel programme experimented by the Church of South India in the 1990s. The activities included regular Bible study and prayer, love-feast and engaging in struggle against unjust systems and practices.

7.15. Trying to change others without changing ourselves amounts to hypocrisy. Liturgical renewal has been talked by many in connection with mission. The way we worship, particularly the Eucharist, proclaims the gospel. As Paul says, 'whenever you eat this bread and drink this cup, you proclaim the Lord's death' (1 Cor. 11: 26). Meaningful songs and prayers ('with spirit and understanding'- 14:15) as well as an orderly performance (14: 40) make a congregation a missionary and evangelical church. And also the way we administer in the church (with love, integrity and servanthood) will reveal to outsiders the kind of God we believe in.

7.16. Checking the menace of fundamentalist and commercialized mission under one person's leadership rests with the churches of a particular area. As history has shown, their emotional manipulation with stylist appearance, voices with particular slang, media glamour and dividing church and creating sect have created missionary competition and confusion. It is a conspiracy that fundamentalists and conservatives (sometimes in combination) call themselves evangelicals and claim what they preach is the true gospel. Church leaders who are theologically sound, instead of using such people in the name of using the gift of the laity, would insist on training and ministering along with the church.

7.17. Thankfully, there are new experiments made by certain individuals and small groups. They identify with the aspirations and suffering of poor victims of injustice in remote villages and tribal areas. While supporting the livelihood of these people they challenge on their behalf rich persons with corrupt business and exploitation of the poor. They lead a sacrificial life and involve in the society risking their own life. It is often suggested that living as a small 'gospel community' in such areas may be more effective. Individual risks will be reduced and organization and administration with the principles of equality and honesty would reflect the beauty and power of the gospel.

8. Christian Hope

8.1. Christian faith is not about gloom and doom and always there is hope for a better future, this is illustrated with a number of stories in the Bible. The basic conviction is that God will never allow his creation to be destroyed. At the same time, he does not interfere in the deliberate choice of people to lose their life or reject to lead a new life. Above all the unfailing love, unfading faithfulness and everlasting compassion of God is the only sources of our hope for the future.

8.2. We read in the creation story, when Adam and Eve crossed the limits set by God by eating the fruit of the tree of good and evil and then was sent out of the garden Eden, the tree of life, the symbol of paradise or life in fullness, was not destroyed. This shows that there was a possibility to come back and participate in the process of recreation (Gen. 3: 24). When everything appeared to be doom and gloom with dried bones God brings new life and humans are called to realise it and participate in spreading the good news of new life and establish structures and symbols of it.

8.3. When Moses was called to liberate the Hebrew slaves from Egypt, God introduced himself as, 'I am the God of Abraham, Isaac and Jacob' (Ex. 3: 16). The tense used here is not past ('was') but present ('am'). Jesus pointed this out to the Sadducees who did not believe in resurrection and ridiculed it by putting forward peculiar stories and questions (Lk. 20: 37). Jesus presents God as the 'Eternal

I am', 'not the God of the dead, but of the living, for to him all are alive' (20: 38).

8.4. Life after death was not the belief given instantly but it was a gradual perception. As far as the early life of the Israelites was concerned, when died, persons joined their ancestors in the grave. Later, here and there are glimpses into life after death and they can be found mainly in the context of undeserved suffering. For example, Job, devout and righteous, when afflicted by calamities and prickling pain in the body, when the wife despised and friends brought forth unhelpful arguments, and even God's role was unclear, expressed his hope in the following words: 'I know that my redeemer lives, and that in the end he will stand on the earth. And after my skin has been destroyed, yet in my flesh I will see God; I myself see him with my own eyes – I, and not another. How my heart yearns within me!' (Job. 19: 25-27).

8.5. More than individual conviction, the Bible portrays collective visions for a golden future. It is difficult to distinguish between the this-worldly hope and other worldly hope. The messianic vision or the peaceable kingdom portrayed in Is. 11 is parabolic and picturesque. A leader with integrity and reconciliation between harmful and harmless creature have the power to kindle imagination and hope. Absence of war, safety, peace and harmony are part of the picture. When their own kings failed them and other kings threatened them it was these visions that sustained peoples' life and hope. Further, from present and parochial purview there is extension to cover the whole universe. Thus, we read heaven and new earth (65: 17-25) in which there will be joy among people in Jerusalem, full longevity of life for all, self-reliance of resources without outside exploitation, harmony and God's intimate presence.

8.6. Ezekiel's vision of the valley of dry bones and the emergence of a new life (Eze. 37) is an acted parable. The prophet had to speak the word of life and breath repeatedly. Also there will be unity in the nation (a united kingdom of Israel and Juda, or northern and southern kingdoms). The original covenant relationship between

God and God's people is the culmination: 'My dwelling place will be with them; I will be their God, and they will be my people. Then the nations will know that I the Lord make Israel holy, when my sanctuary is among them forever' (v. 27-28). In the whole of the Bible there is no heaven greater than the living presence of God.

8.7. Following political depression (under Greek rulers), persecution and coming of the Son of Man in solidarity with the victims, there is a beautiful vision of the end times in Dan. 12. Following the mention of the archangel Michael and book of life, the resurrection of the martyrs are described in a glorious picture: 'Multitudes who sleep in the dust of the earth will awake: some to everlasting life, others to shame and everlasting contempt. Those who are wise will shine like the brightness of the heavens, and those who lead many to righteousness, like the stars forever and ever' (v. 2-3).

8.8. Jesus' teaching of end times is not systematic and consistent. On the one hand, he exhorted not to discriminate crops and weeds but on the other told that at the time of harvest the weeds will be bundled and burned (Mt. 13: 29-30). He told the disciples 'judge not lest you be judge' (7: 1) but he was judging the corrupt rulers, hypocritically religious and conservative wings of the Jews. He encouraged his disciples saying, 'Do not be afraid of those who kill the body but cannot kill the soul. Rather, be afraid of the One who can destroy both soul and body in hell' (10: 28).

8.9. Jesus was speaking about the kingdom of God or heaven both in terms of here and now and here after. In the coming of Jesus, the kingdom came near people, particularly the poor and victims of injustice, which was a good news to them (Mk. 1: 15; Lk. 10: 9, 11). All that Jesus said and did centred around the inbreaking of this new reality which influenced people and the society just like salt and yeast. But those who identified the kingdom of God with a political reality of freedom from foreign forces asked, when the kingdom of God would come? Jesus replied, 'The coming of the kingdom of God is not something that can be observed, nor will people say, "Here it is," or "There it is," because the kingdom of God is in your midst'

(Lk. 17: 20-21). While on trial, Jesus told Pilate, 'my kingdom is not of this world' (Jn. 1: 36). This does not mean that Jesus' kingdom is otherworldly but that it is qualitatively different from the world the politics of which is tainted by unjust hierarchy, violence and exploitation. But did Jesus expect that the kingdom of God would be established in his life time? He did speak about the distant future, heavenly feast and judgment (Mt. 8: 11-12; Mk. 14: 25).

8.10. Though all his disciples and those who believed them were supposed to do their duty without any expectation of reward, Jesus did speak about it. Thus, he promised those who were persecuted because of him Jesus said, 'Rejoice and be glad, because great is your reward in heaven' (Mt. 5: 12). When his disciples asked for the reward of leaving everything and following him, Jesus promised that they would receive hundred times as much and inherit eternal life' (19: 29). When the seventy-two disciples returned with joy and said, 'Lord, even the demons submit to us in your name' Jesus told them, 'do not rejoice that the spirits submit to you, but rejoice that your names are written in heaven' (Lk. 10: 17, 20).

8.11. While Jesus was sharing the popular Jewish beliefs in soul (or life force), judgement, heaven and hell, the most shocking element in his teaching was the possibility of self-deception and surprise. For example, he said 'on that day' many will come and say that they have prophesied, driven out demons and performed miracles in his name, but he will say plainly, 'I never knew you. Away from me, you evildoers' (Mt. 7: 22-23). And in the parable of the coming of the Son of Man in glory, he will sit on his throne and judge between sheep and goats, and pronounced that blessed are those who feed the hungry, give drink to the thirst, invite the stranger in, clothe the naked, look after the ill and visit the prison. Both groups asked the same question: 'when did we see you in this condition? Jesus' answer was, 'whatever you did (or did not) for one of the least of these brothers and sisters of mine, you did for me. Thus, the righteous who helped the needy without knowing that they helped Jesus (Jesus was always in solidarity with the needy) went to eternal life and others to eternal punishment (25: 31-46). What a surprise and warning!

8.12. Certain clusters of sayings by Jesus can be easily misunderstood if they are not carefully read with reference to the historic context. Let us take, for example, Mark, chapter 13. The cluster has baffled devout readers as well as scholars as to its context and purpose. If we take the messages of the text as they appear, the following can be noted. First, Jesus foretold the destruction of the temple at Jerusalem which happened in 70 CE. This is followed by a prediction of persecution of his disciples (perhaps the Marcan community) and encouraging and comforting words. While the exact nature and character of Messiah was unclear, in future many will come with the claim that they were Christ (Messiah), prophets or those who came in his name. This also happened as indicated elsewhere (Acts 5: 36-37). There is prediction of war, uprisings, earth quakes and famines, along with sufferings for the disciples. Though there is an element of last stage of the present world's existence, such things have happened with panic calls since the time of Jesus. Hostility within family too has been noticed. The reader is asked to understand 'the abomination that causes desolation' which refers to the pagan altar erected in the Jerusalem temple by the Greek rulers in the 2nd century BCE (Dan. 9: 27; 11: 31; 12: 11). If we imagine the destruction of the temple by the order of the Roman emperor it was he who was the abomination although people feared mentioning it openly as the punishment would be death. Then there is a transition to a blend of cosmic signs (darkening of sun and moon) and shakening of the heavenly bodies including stars, and the victorious coming of the Son of Man in clouds. The 'Son of Man' refers to Dan. 7: 14 where he demonstrated his solidarity with the victims of persecution. The natural process of the growth of the fig tree is compared to the coming of the Son of Man. But no one except the Father knows the time of end and therefore the readers are asked to keep watch. On the whole past, present and future are combined in the text (Mk. 13).

8.13. If Jesus expected his kingdom fully established in his own life, his mission was a failure. Then we can understand that the enthusiastic disciple Judas, when that did not happen when Jesus was to be executed, killed himself. And Jesus' saying that 'The one who believes in me will live, even though they die; and whoever lives by believing in me will never die' (Jn. 11: 25) seems to suggest that Jesus was open to possibilities, not with certainties of details. In any case, even on the cross, in response to the prayer of a criminal ('remember me when you come into your kingdom'), Jesus replied, 'you will be with me in paradise' (Lk. 23: 42-43). According to Peter, Jesus, soon after his death was made alive in the Spirit, went and proclaimed to the imprisoned spirits of the flood of Noah's time, thus making an extraordinary note of his grace (1Pet. 3: 19-20). Further, just before his ascension, the disciples asked Jesus, 'Lord, are you at this time going to restore the kingdom to Israel?' They were keen to have the promised honour of sitting on twelve thrones to judge the 12 tribes of Israel. Jesus' replied: 'It is not for you to know the times or the dates of the Father has set by his own authority…but you will be witnesses' (Acts 1: 6-8). This is consistent with his earlier teaching that his disciples (all Christians) should not worry about the time of the end but engage in transforming the world.

8.14. Apostles' descriptions about the last days, second coming of Jesus, their awaiting his arrival in their own times are bitty and fragmented. Paul mentions that God has a day when he will judge the world with justice by the man (Jesus) he has appointed (17: 31). But in an astonishing passage he presents the whole creation groaning for salvation along with the children of God. 'For in this hope we were saved. But hope that is seen is not hope at all. Who hopes for what they already have? But if we hope for what we do not yet have we wait for it patiently' (Rom. 8: 22-25). He has a long description of God's wrath and judgment against sinful humanity, probably addressing a particular context (1: 18-2: 16). Later, he writes: 'Be joyful in hope, patient in affliction, faithful in prayer' (12: 12). For him, 'the kingdom of God is not a matter of eating and drinking, but of righteousness, peace and joy in the Holy Spirit'

(14: 17). (Earlier we saw that Jesus expected eating and drinking in the kingdom!). As if slightly revising Jesus' words Paul tells the Romans to understand the present time: 'The hour has already come for you to wake up from your slumber because our salvation is nearer now than when we first believed. The night is nearly over; the day is almost here' (13: 11-12). As a Pharisee, Paul shared the belief in resurrection. In the context of describing this in the life experience of believers, he provides a profound vision of the end times. It includes the coming of Chris and, the coming together of those who belonged to him. 'Then the end will come, when he hands over the kingdom to God the Father after he has destroyed all dominion, authority and power. (He will subdue all enemies including the death under his feet). 'When he has done this, then the Son himself will be made subject to God who put everything under him so that God may be all in all' (1 Cor. 15: 23-28). We are in a perpetual process of glorious transformation while awaiting the heavenly home, glorified body and judgment seat but with confidence (2 Cor. 3: 16f; 5: 1-10). Moreover, by pastoral admonition he narrates the coming of the Lord from heaven 'with a loud command, with the voice of the archangel and with the trumpet call of God, and the dead in Christ will rise first. After that, we who are still alive and are left will be caught up together with them in the clouds to meet the Lord in the air and so we will be with the Lord forever' (1Thes. 4: 16-17). The warning continues with the note of unknowability of the day and time of the Lord who will come as a thief, and the need of living as children of light (5: 2-10). In another picture, he says that the Lord Jesus will be revealed from heaven in blazing fire with his powerful angels and judgment for the wicked (2 Thes. 1: 7-10). It is obvious that Paul had a changing understanding of the last things and he did not worry about consistency. In any case, there is no room for abdicating responsibilities to preserve God's creation or supporting nuclear wars with a view to speed of the end of the world. The judgment will be on the basis of what we have done to save the creation even if in the end humanity will destroy it!

8.15. Peter gives a different portrayal of the day of the Lord. It includes the emergence of the scoffers, destruction of the present heavens and earth by fire, day of judgment for the ungodly, God's time being different from ours (a day is like a thousand years) the Lord's patience for everyone to come to repentance and coming of the day like a thief. Therefore, he adds, God's children should be holy and spotless looking for the coming of God. God's patience is our salvation. Peter's reference to Paul's writing on this matter (perhaps not included in the NT) and the fact that it was hard to understand which the ignorant and unstable people distort, as they do the other scriptures, to their own destruction, calls for reverential consideration (2 Pet. 3: 3-16).

8.16. John warns against the denial of Son and the Father by anti-Christ in the last hour (1 Jn. 2: 22f). He brings again his favourite teaching that we have the authority to be the children of God. There, addressing a confused situation about the last day or end time, he writes: 'Dear friends, now we are children of God, and what we will be has not yet been made known. But we know that when Christ appears, we shall be like him, for we shall see him as he is' (3: 2).

8.17. The apocalyptic images of the last book of the Bible needs to be approached very carefully. Its background was the seven churches of Asia Minor which were persecuted by Rome because of their challenging mission against the imperial cult and all exploitation therewith. The flashing images of the fights and wars between a vulnerable Lamb and wild beasts end in the victory of the Lamb and his followers who suffered persecution and were given a reassurance of new life and new world. There is mention of a declaration that 'blessed are the dead who die in the Lord from now on. They will rest from their labour for their deeds will follow them' (Rev. 14: 13). There is a first resurrection for martyrs who will reign with Christ for thousand years (20: 4-6). The last two chapters (21-22) mention the appearance of new heaven and new earth, the confession that God's dwelling place is among the people, the new Jerusalem coming down out of heaven from God as ever lightful with gates always un-shut,

Lamb's book of life, the kings of the earth bringing their splendor into it, and a garden with herbal trees with healing potency and a river with crystal clear water, reflecting the original garden of Eden. No more pain and suffering!

8.18. On the whole, if we take all the sayings and picturesque images of the last things literally, we will stumble. Normally fundamentalist preachers point out those texts which work in favour of their vested interest. Misunderstanding and misinterpretation are well acknowledged in the Bible. There are no doctrines in the sayings or writings of Jesus and Paul. All we can say for certain is that in the scripture there are visions but not a blueprint. Godfearing people and disciples of Jesus have much to learn from these visions for a faithful commitment, holy life and dedicated engagement in transforming mission.

8.19. History of Christianity has recorded many preachers who fixed a date for the second coming of Jesus and caused his followers to sell their property etc. When nothing happened they gave curious and strange interpretations. We have already mentioned Jim Jones. More recently, at the dawn of the new millennium (2000) a group of Americans who were convinced that the Lord was coming and descending upon the Mount Olive, were waiting. But in conversation, a journalist found out from them that all had the return tickets to fly home! In India the caption 'Christ is coming soon' goes with fundamentalist preaching and publicity. But when they ask for donations to build strong buildings with attractive promises of this-worldly blessings, ignorant and gullible people give generously while intelligent people question!

9. Interfaith Relations and Dialogue

9.1. Many Christians continue to be hesitant to take people of other faiths positively and suspect the aims and fruits of dialogue with them but they have good friends, meet friendly people in travel, in living and working places. There are stories of interfaith blood donation and taking risk to protect persons of other faiths during trouble.

9.2. To label interfaith dialogue 'a satanic movement' shows one's ignorance. Throughout the Bible there are interreligious encounters which resulted in both positively and negatively. Some western missionaries who came to India with a single aim to preach the gospel and convert the pagan natives, went through a new conversion themselves. They enjoyed the welcome and hospitality of Buddhists, Hindus, Muslims and Sikhs. They took pains to study their religions and present them objectively. Some advocated a new approach to people of other faiths with 'justice, courtesy and love' as there are valuable visions and experiences of God and exemplary ethical values.

9.3. As we see in the Bible, the 'people of God' encountered many 'peoples of God,' who were good and god-fearing. Abraham found god-fearing among the people of Abimelek including their king (Gen. 20: 11). Two Egyptian midwives belied the Pharaoh's order and spared the life of the baby Moses for they had fear of God and God blessed them (Ex. 1: 17-20). Such recognition continued in the New Testament. Peter was led to encounter the 'devout and God-fearing' Cornelius, a centurion of Italian regiment and his family. His message opened with the declaration that 'I now realise how true it is that God does not show favouritism but accepts from every nation the one who fears him and does what is right' (Acts 10: 34-35).

9.4. Affirmation of the creation of the world, sustenance of life and of the universal witness was the preamble to the gospel. Paul in Lystra declared God's universal creation and added, 'In the past, he let all the nations go their own way. Yet he has not left himself without testimony' by giving food and all seasonal gifts (Acts 14: 15-18; he echoes what Jesus pointed out that the heavenly Father gives sun and rain to both righteous and the wicked – Mt. 5: 45-48). In Athens he starts his speech with such affirmation (Acts 17: 24-2). James also declares that every good and perfect gift comes from God, the father of the heavenly lights (Js. 1: 17). Paul writes to the Gentile Romans that equivalent to the Hebrew law, the requirements of the same are written in their hearts and, their consciences also bearing witness (Ro. 2: 12-15).

9.5. The name of Elijah is connected with some wonderful individuals from other religions and cultures. On the one hand, he was a champion of justice and opposed the Baal worship which was tainted with cruel forms of idol worship, obscene fertility rites and injustice, and which was promoted by Jezebel the foreign wife of the Israelite king Ahab (e.g. 1Kgs. 18, 21). On the other hand, when he was rejected by his own people, as Jesus pointed out that though there were many widows among Israel, Elijah was not sent to any of them, but to a widow in Zarephath (Lk. 4: 24-26; cf. 1Kgs. 17: 7-24). Elijah's follower Elisha, expressed his magnanimity towards Naaman of Syria whom he had healed of leprosy. When the Syrian commander asked forgiveness for having to bow down in the temple of Rimmon while accompanying his Master, Elisha said, 'Go in peace' (Kgs. 5: 18-19). In the nomadic or wandering life in ancient Israel, presumably such positive encounters were common.

9.6. In eighth century (BCE) Israel was in crossroads having to solve conflicts and ensure peace while being sandwiched by two empires.

In a stunning forecast Isaiah portrayed an unbelievable picture in which the archenemies Assyria and Egypt shared God's blessing while Israel continued to be God's inheritance (Is. 19: 23-25). Through Amos God declared that not only Israel but also Cushites (people from upper Nile region), Philistines and Arameans were led to liberation by God (Amos 9: 7). While the expectation of Zion as the destination of all nations where they will be judged persisted thus encouraging the later Zionist movement (Is. 2: 2; Mic. 4: 2), Micah envisioned peaceful co-existence and communal harmony without any threat. He added a theological note of tolerance: 'All the nations may walk in the name of their gods, but we will walk in the name of the Lord our God for ever and ever' (Mic. 4: 5).

9.7. While people were expecting the Messiah in the line of David (Is. 11: 1), the line was snapped by a new perception. The Persian king Cyrus who released the captives from Judea in Babylon, to return to and rebuild Jerusalem in the 6th century BCE, an alien who worshipped his gods and goddesses, was projected as Messiah by the (second) Isaiah (45). Cyrus is described as the anointed, the one led by God's hand, given victory over nations and so on. This intervention brought enduring changes in the understanding of Messiah.

9.8. In the story of Jonah, God and the innocent people of Nineveh repented but Jonah, the servant of God, failed to see that his co-passengers in the ship were more devout and humane, and the God all-compassionate changed his mind to destroy the people when they all, including the king and cattle, sat in ashes in penitence.

9.9. The book of Ruth supports interfaith and intercultural marriage and the outcome affected the genealogy of Jesus. There are four foreign women mentioned in the genealogy of Jesus (Tamar, Rahab, Ruth and (Bathsheba) Uriah's wife (Mt. 1: 3-6). Presumably, Matthew was countering the notion of 'pure blood' or pure race.

9.10. Jesus' encounter with the Samaritan woman at a well was remarkable as there was so much hostility between the Jews and the Samaritans. The conversation started with Jesus' asking her for water and mutual exchange and progressive development led them to recognize new aspects of truth. No more in Jerusalem and the Samaritan mountain, in the coming time, people will worship God everywhere and most essential was worshipping God in spirit and truth. Finally, the woman mentioned the expectation for the Messiah, Jesus indicated that he was the one to come and belief of many Samaritans (Jn. 4).

9.11. Jesus appreciated the 'faith' (not a religious belief, but capacity to transcend or move on) of a centurion (Mt. 8: 5-13), a Canaanite woman (15: 21-28) and a Samaritan (Lk. 17: 11-19). The centurion found himself unworthy to receive Jesus into his house because he did not fit into the power structure of Rome. This is more than simple humility. The Canaanite woman was persistent to challenge Jesus to widen the boundary of his mission. The Samaritan, who had been miraculously cured of leprosy along with nine other Jews, came back to Jesus and thanked him. In all these three encounters, the extraordinary definition of faith is applied to people of other faiths. It is worth noting that, following the encounter with a centurion, Jesus said that 'many will come from the east and the west, and will take their places at the feast with Abraham, Isaac and Jacob in the kingdom of heaven. But the subjects of the kingdom will be thrown outside, into the darkness, where there will be weeping and gnashing of teeth' (Mt. 8: 11-12).

9.12. Once the disciples reported to Jesus that they had seen someone driving out demons in his name and tried to stop him. Jesus asked them not to stop him and said, 'for whoever is not against you is for you' (Lk. 9: 49f). Non-Christian contributions towards the reign of God and its justice are considerable throughout centuries. Individuals with sacrificial commitment are engaged in actions of liberation and reconstruction among the victims of injustice and exploitation in India. Mere 'name' does not matter as has been already noted.

9.13. In every religious text there are exclusive claims and those who take them literally may become fanatics. In Christians circles passages such as Jn. 14: 6 and 4: 12 are interpreted that way. We need to know the real meaning. For example, in response to a question Jesus said, 'I am the way, truth and life' in a context where many claimed themselves as messiahs. *Way* does not mean shortcut, nor a broad way, but it is the way of suffering. There is no sense of a physical distance between the heavenly Father and people and needed was a spiritual insight into the heart of God which is wounded and bleeding for the victims of injustice and the suffering. *Truth* here does not mean an abstract concept, nor a doctrinal capsule. Jesus told Pilate that he had come to witness to the truth. For Jesus truth was the reign of God breaking into the world and those called by God were to be open to its unfolding and manifestation. The truth sets us free. Jesus embodied this concrete truth. *Life* does not mean the combination of prosperity, protection, progeny, popularity, promotion and peace of mind. Jesus said that he had come to seek and find the lost and last sheep and was ready to give his life for them. He came to give life in its fullness. Meaningful life is life-giving, life-saving and life-affirming for all. Similarly, the confession 'only name of Jesus for salvation' has a context, i.e. the healing of a cripple and questioning of the temple authorities 'in whose name and power?' When we liberate the disabled and the downtrodden and others ask such questions we should answer in the apostles' way.

9.14. This is not to shy away from our responsibility to share the good news of Jesus Christ, nor to deny the unique insights of the gospel. Love is the key and surrendering to be governed by the crucified centre is the basis of the Christian life. Arrogance and aggressiveness is the enemy of the gospel. Christians have lived along with people of other faiths with cordial and friendly contacts in many cases. They watch our worship and life. We have many opportunities to share the gospel insights; particularly to defend our hope, but with 'gentleness and respect' (1Pet. 3: 15). Thus, we stimulate a life of dialogue with commitment and openness.

9.15. Missionaries encountering world religions and their change of attitude and approach to people of other faiths have already been noted. Such missionary experiences contributed to serious discussions about the relationship between Christians and people of other faiths in mission conferences and general assemblies of the World Council of Churches. Guidelines have been produced and Christians are encouraged to maintain good relationship with the neighbours of others faiths. It is understood that Christians have to reflect with prayer relevant understanding of theology without bearing false witness against their neighbours.

9.16. Interfaith dialogue greatly helps to understand what others believe and practice and to clarify any misunderstanding about the Christian faith. Those Christian ministers of dialogue are often astonished, even shocked, to know how others understand Christianity. For example, an average Hindu thinks that Jesus is the personal deity of Christians who worship him in their temples (churches) with the help of their 'priests' with a view to get rich blessings including to get the soul into eternal rest. Well informed Muslims and Jews think that Christians commit the unforgivable sin of worshipping prophet Jesus as God. Persons from Buddhist, Jain and Sikh traditions too pose challenges to the way Christians worship, live and preach. Those committed to share the uniqueness of the Christian faith would immediately recognize the need of new reformation in India which would include terminological and structural changes.

9.17. Christians are a tiny minority in multifaith and secular India. It is often pointed out that Christians along with people of other religious and secular communities should feel obliged to work for the integrity and development of the nation. Sometimes we may confront those who justify the age long evils of discriminatory caste and untouchability, poverty, corruption, human rights violations against women, children, disabled, third genders etc. If every church/ diocese has trained personnel in social engagement and interfaith dialogue that will show our sincere commitment to the welfare of the nation.

9.18. The Indian Constitution provides the fundamental right to profess, practice and propagate one's religion. But there is a conditional clause, i.e., 'public order, health and morality.' Thus, we have both a privilege and responsibility.

9.19. Christian faith and life is a continuing journey and we are not expected to tarry on the way with a claim of a package of truths and perfection. The Deuteronomist wisdom is relevant for all: 'The secret things belong to the Lord our God, but the things revealed belong to us and to our children forever, that we may follow all the words of this law' (29: 29). Jesus asked us to grow towards perfection (maturity and generosity) of the heavenly Father (Mt. 5: 48). For Paul, knowledge of Christ in flesh is not enough and he commits to an ongoing process of knowing the living Christ (Phil. 3: 12-14). Elsewhere the apostle explains the purpose of prayer 'to grasp how wide and long and high and deep is the love of Christ, and to know this love that surpasses knowledge – that you may be filled to the measure of all the fullness of God' (Eph. 3: 18-21). Those who meditate intently on this process and progress may spontaneously become gently, generous, humble and gracious, with fascinating charm that may influence others in contact.

9.20. How to assess the effect and benefits of science and secularism? For example, does the theory of evolution essentially deny the belief in God's creation? There are those who have strong belief in God but also believes in God's discreet presence and creativity in the evolution and scientific developments. At the same time, they are critical of the use of scientific progress for destructive purposes. Similarly, secular visions and ideas have helped to purge religion of its excess and lopsidedness, such as superstition, war and denominational/sectarian conflicts. The question asked is, can there be a secularism without implicit faith or religiosity? What are the different expressions of secular faith in different countries? What is the specific nature of secularism in multifaith India? Such questions are important not only for Christians but also people of other faiths. Therefore, it will be a worthwhile exercise to discuss them as interreligious groups.

10. Theological Education in India

10.1. Christian life and history on the whole has not been averse to wisdom, knowledge and intellectual pursuit. The 'Proverbs' praise knowledge and wisdom but warns against misuse. 'The fear of the Lord is the beginning of knowledge, but fools despise wisdom and instruction' (Pro. 1: 7). The expected Messiah was to be endowed with the Spirit of wisdom, understanding, knowledge and fear of God (Is. 11: 2-3). But knowledge and wisdom can drift to craftiness which could be used for the fulfilment of vested interest, which leads to degradation of society or nation.

10.2. The twin commandment of loving God with all our heart, mind, soul and strength, and loving our neighbours as ourselves has the component of mind or reasoning lest love urns to be sentimental and emotional. An integrated spirituality combining devotion, reason and action is healthy and useful. We have a tradition of saints who lived with this balance. Normally, the dull-headed and mediocre ridicule intelligence and critical thinking with a view to justify their position and convince people.

10.3. Jesus had a funny band of disciples and he often chided them as dull-headed, forgetful, power mongering, timid and un-understanding. For more than three years he tried to train them and transform them from 'wholly fools to holy fools.' When he sent them on mission among wolves, his advice was 'be as shrewd as snakes and as innocent as doves' (Mt. 10: 16). In extremes, serpent can be crafty and dove gullible. But Jesus meant being intelligent and innocent. Also, Jesus warned them against religious teachers of the law. 'They like to walk around in flowing robes and love to be greeted with respect in the market-places and have the most important seats in the synagogues and the places of honour at banquets. They devour widows' houses and for a show make lengthy prayers. These men will be punished most severely' (Lk. 20: 46-7). There are church traditions which follow simple uniforms for their ministers and prescribe short and meaningful prayers.

10.4. It was Paul who with intelligence and education made a distinction between the real fools for the world's sake and realized fools for Christ's sake. His central message was that the crucified God (the cross of Jesus) made the wisdom of the world foolish. In the context of sign-seeking Jews and wisdom-seeking Greeks, he says, 'bur we preach Christ crucified: a stumbling-block to Jews and foolishness to Gentiles, but to those whom God has called, both Jews and Greeks, Christ the power of God and the wisdom of God' (1Cor. 1: 23-24). Recognizing the different caliber of Paul, Peter observed that some of his writings were hard to understand which ignorant and unstable people distort (2 Pet. 3: 15-16).

10.5. Paul would not accept that Christians remove their brain for a while when they went in to worship. We have already noted his exhortation to the chaotic church in Corinth. He criticized some people who were talking smooth and flattery, thus deceiving the mind of naïve people (Rom. 16: 19). He clarifies that in his proclamation of God, he was admonishing and teaching everyone with all wisdom so that everyone may be presented fully mature in Christ (Col. 1: 28). 'Then we will no longer be infants, tossed back and forth by the waves, and blown here and there by every wind of teaching and by the cunning and craftiness of people in their deceitful scheming' (Eph. 4: 14). Instead, speaking the truth in love, we would lead to growing into maturity. Paul warns against false teachers who had no understanding but unhealthy interest in controversies and competitions (1Tim. 6: 4-5; for more details of the false teachers, see 2 Tim. 2: 14-19). Further, Paul predicts a time when 'people will not put up with sound doctrine. Instead, to suit their own desires they will gather teachers 'to say what their itching ears want to hear. They will turn their ears away from the truth and turn aside to myths' (2 Tim. 4: 3-4). With the benefits of globalization and media glamour some of such teachers and preachers have scaled a great height of commercial success in India.

10.6. Most fundamentalist preachers claimed to be inspired concurrently by the Holy Spirit. Therefore they openly ridicule any systematic theological education and ministerial training. Where there are training camps organized by the successful and popular preachers, they give more importance to style, not substance. Many point out that as Jesus has said to his disciples they need not worry about what to speak and the Spirit will speak through them. Obviously, the concerned saying of Jesus they have misunderstood. Jesus said this in connection with persecution when rulers and authorities arrest them and put on trial. 'When they arrest you, do not worry about what to say or how to say it. At that time you will be given what to say, for it will not be you speaking, but the Spirit of your Father speaking through you' (Mt. 10: 18-20). This misuse is one example of many which make theological education indispensable.

10.7. Early Church Councils were organized in order to settle controversies. The first council that met in Jerusalem (Acts 15) debated and decided on the question of the Gentile Christians having to follow the Jewish customs such as circumcision. The decision was that they need not observe them except abstaining from food sacrificed to idols, blood, the meat of strangled animals and sexual immorality. It was communicated to the concerned churches by a letter. This is the only council recorded in the New Testament. Further councils, judged some teachings and movements heretic, produced the two creeds and set of doctrines. Some church fathers contributed to the finalization of the New Testament and wrote books expounding the doctrines. Though the doctrines were seen as set in stone and sealed in steel boxes, from today's context and contextual reading of the Bible one can find in them many shortcomings.

10.8. There was much of devotional and intellectual activities in the monasteries. It is important to note that Martin Luther (1483-1546) was an Augustinian friar and lived in a monastery. In the wake of renaissance and small attempts of reformation he re-read his Bible most intently. He found the Catholic Church based in Rome as not taking the scripture seriously and practicing unbiblical acts such as the indulgence. His confrontation with Rome resulted in excommunication. He and his fellow reformers (e.g. John Calvin and Huldrych Zwingli) reinterpreted the traditional doctrines though there was no unanimity about issues such as the structure and governance of the church. Hence the emergence of denominations. Theological studies in the Protestant church were held in small scale. In due course, there were full-fledged theological colleges/seminaries and Bible Schools. Soon departments of theology originated in secular and church-based universities where one can do a degree course. In some cases, students worked for the university degree while being resident in their denominational colleges for pastoral studies and practical work. Missionaries were keen to establish institutions for theological education and ministerial training.

10.9. William Carey, the great Baptist missionary from England, arrived in Kolkota (then Calcutta) in 1793 which was the headquarters of the British East India Company. Experiencing unwelcome, he moved to northern Bengal and worked as an indigo planter. In 1799, he was followed by Johsua Marshman and William Ward and in 1800 was induced to join them in Serampore, a Danish settlement, 20 miles north of Kolkota. With burning interest in parting education to the locals, following establishing forty-five schools in and around Serampore, they founded the Serampore College in 1818. It was for the 'training of Indian and European youth in Eastern and Western Science and Literature (which) may be regarded as the crown of their educational activities and aims.' Divinity was added as a 'boarding department for Europeans and Indian Christians in training for missionary and other work.' Carey was gifted in learning and teaching languages such as Bengali and Sanskrit and gradually translated the Bible, part or whole, in almost all the north Indian languages. He as a part time Professor of Fort William College and his colleagues working in printing etc., it is remarkable to note that the Serampore Trio, earned their own income and was not paid by the mission. Moreover, their interaction and dialogue with the 'Calcutta thinkers' (e.g. Ram Mohun Roy), reveal their bold attempts, but betrayed the failure of an approach governed by doctrines and denominational rigidity.

10.10. The Serampore College was incorporated by a Danish Royal Charter in 1829. And it was one of the first Colleges to be affiliated to the University of Calcutta established in 1857. 'The Higher Theological Department since its reorganization alongside of the Arts and Vernacular Theological Departments' was expanded in 1911. The Charter was revived under the Bengal Act of 1918 and later modified by the Government. Since then six colleges or seminaries were affiliated and the number has increased to fifty-five plus five specialist centres (2017). There have been a number of degree programmes and diplomas and the history of revisions is astonishing. Just as the Serampore Trio affirmed, church leaders and informed leaders in India openly acknowledge that it has been God's doing within mission.

10.11. Personal formation, theological formation and ministerial formation are taken as key by seminaries/colleges affiliated to the Senate of Serampore College (University). The curriculum is supposed to take care of study, practical work, engagement with churches and exposures to the ecumenical environments. There are efforts to keep theology as an integral discipline striking the right balance. Conservative trends and fundamentalist forces which try to influence the programmes is a constant challenge.

10.12. It is important to ensure that those who come to theological education and ministerial training have personal integrity and right intention. If picking up things with un-interest and getting a degree as a professional qualification with a misplaced confidence that churches can be easily managed by blindly following the tradition, the outcome is wastage. It is often pointed out that theologians and theological students, first and foremost, must be sure of the fundamental command they follow: love God with all our being, and love others as ourselves. If so, they cannot neglect the prayers in the chapel because even if what happen there is not always interesting, the very fact of sitting in God's presence and in solidarity with the fellow theologians should be seen as significant. It should be seen as minimum expression of the love for God and fellow believers in a community. This will reduce the agony of the Principals and Chaplains as well!

10.13. If all our prayers and studies are geared to being rooted and established in love, grasping its length, height, depth and width, and growing towards the fullness of God (Eph. 3: 14ff), theological education becomes transforming lives and reforming churches.

10.14. However, theological illiteracy and confusion continue; we are not able to check the influence of fundamentalist groups and elicit openness from the conservative churches. More important is that if the church leaders do not work in close association with theologians and theological colleges, unnecessary tension will continue. When a church leader publicly tells their candidates in training, 'return just as you joined and leave all that you learned in the campus' it is not only ridiculing faith, education and training, but also a mockery faith.

10.15. However, we have theologically qualified ministers and their number increases. But compared to developments in other qualifications, theological qualification remains unused while there is some respect for the titles and degrees. There has been a mushroom growth of some sort of hon. Drs. that eclipses the earned degrees including doctorate. Church leaders have a significant role to play to recognize authentic titles, integrate new theological insights into the life and ministry of the churches.

10.16. There has been a mushrooming of fundamentalist Bible schools. Though they appear to be open and even able to work out affiliation with respected universities, their life style, spirituality and methods of missionary outreach are hardly sensitive to the context, condition and commitment of the people who they target for conversion. It is obvious that 'He who pays gets his music played' and it suggests their fundamentalist sponsors from wealthy countries.

10.17. Without undermining the freedom of individual institutions, but recognizing the continued confusion about fundamental themes such as salvation and priesthood of all believers, there should be statements of understanding and clear guidelines for the churches.

10.18. Terminological confusion has to be removed by explaining terms such as liberal, evangelical, ecumenical, radical, and continued reformation. For example, 'evangelical' is a beautiful term meaning 'being good news' or 'bearing good news.' Many Protestant Churches around the world have this term as an adjective to the name of their Church. Fundamentalist groups by a conspiracy have claimed it to be their own, and churches and Christians in the English-speaking world have been carried away by this identification. Likewise, liberals are wooly and non-committal but those who work for the liberation of victims from oppressive forces are clear in thinking and committed in action.

10.19. Paradigm shifts through experiments need to be happening in ministry and theological education. A reflective praxis is the need of the hour. This may happen in two ways. First, what students encounter in churches of their concurrent placement should be shared and discussed in the college. They should be encouraged to assess the gap between what they are taught and what they see in the churches. Second, at least for a year in their ministry, the former students should maintain a journal and come for a seminar to discuss with teachers in the seminary. The arrangement needs the co-operation of the church leaders. In both cases, teachers should be expected to write their own reflection about the relevance of their teaching and the existing curriculum.

10.20. In most cases young ministers who are fresh from the seminaries want to experiment with new liturgies and new forms of ministry. But their church leaders who are not theologically enlightened and spiritually matured, discourage them and label them rebels and even punish them in subtle ways. If theological education is accepted as sleeveless learning, there may be possibilities for the leaders, ministers and congregations learning together. Such joint refresher courses may be resourced by teachers from the seminaries and in turn they will be able to feed back to their institution.

10.21. Lay theological education is extremely important. As Paul says, all forms of ministry is 'to prepare God's people' (Eph. 4: 12f). 'Ministry by People' has an ecumenical focus and several experiments have been made to equip members of congregations in their living contexts. But in India we do not have opportunities to know these experiments and their effects in church life and witness. Surely each centre has valuable lessons and insights to share with others.

10.22. While being open to insights from lived discipleship and shared in solidarity anywhere in the world, we should not believe the myth that materials produced in English by western scholars are of more authentic and superior quality. Academic theology that emerges in university departments without any care for the churches declining, however sophisticated, should be critically looked at. Even the ministry of interfaith dialogue suffers from arid theories worked out elsewhere which have no relevance in the unique context of India. At the same time, original theological text-books must be produced in India.

10.23. The Senate of Serampore College has a programme of theological text-books, and through workshops guidelines have been prepared. There are bursaries provided. Writers are encouraged to produce standard text-books in the vernacular. Besides, considerable amount of light-weight theological literature is available for the laity. However, those who are carried away by fundamentalism are yet to be convinced about the importance of proper approach to the Bible, church and mission. Perhaps there may be an external committee to evaluate the standard and style of the existing literature and to recommend new literature in order to reach the unreached.

10.24. The Senate may have to come up with a declaration that fundamentalism in any form – literal interpretation of certain favourite passages of the scripture, abstinence from engaging in mission of solidarity with the victims (not simple charity), verbal militancy, personality cult with media glamour, sectarianism and interpretation of blessing as mammon, progeny and popularity, salvation of soul for next world through the blood of Jesus – is the enemy of the gospel, confusing mission and damaging Christian witness in India. If not already there, it is high time to come up with a basic theological statement, which may be shared by all the theological colleges.

Participants – Principals and Heads of Institutions

1. Dr. K. David Udayakumar, Gurukul Lutheran Theological College & Research Institute, Chennai
2. Dr. Sunil Michael Caleb, Bishop's College, Kolkata
3. Dr. Limatula Longkumer, Registrar, NIIGTS, Kolkata
4. Rev. Johnson Sundara Raj, Allahabad Bible Seminary, Allahabad
5. Dr. Yesudian Vijaysingh, Bethel Bible Institute, Danishpet
6. Dr. Mathew Emmanuel Tatapudi, Andhra Christian Theological College, Hyderabad
7. Dr. I. P. Asheervadam, Mennonite Brethren Centenary Bible College, Hyderabad
8. Rev. Arpan Christian, Methodist Bible Seminary, Vasad
9. Rev. Ms. Sonal Christian, United Theological Seminary of Maharashtra, Pune
10. Dr. Packiam T. Samuel, Henry Martyn Institute, Hyderabad
11. Dr. Watson, Karnataka Theological College, Mangalore (Rep.)
12. Dr. Vasantha Rao, Andhra Christian Theological College, Hyderabad (Guest)
13. Dr. H. G. Mithra, Union Biblical Seminary, Pune; Secretary, ATTI (Organiser)
14. Dr. Israel Selvanayagam, Gurukul Lutheran Theological College & Research Institute, Chennai; President, ATTI (Main Resource Person)